IF WE STICK TOGETHER...

IF WE STICK TOGETHER...

Advantage
BOOKS

Michael La Sage

If We Stick Together by Michael La Sage
Copyright © 2021 by Michael La Sage
All Rights Reserved.
ISBN: 978-1-59755-635-4

Published by: ADVANTAGE BOOKS™
                    Longwood, FL
                    www.advbookstore.com

Library of Congress Catalog Number: 2021937610

Names:	La Sage, Michael, Author
Title:	If We Stick Together / Michael La Sage
Description	Longwood: Advantage Books, 2021
Identifiers:	ISBN (print): 9781597556354, (mobi, epub): 9781597556477 Subjects: Parenting & Relationships: Family Relationships – Abuse, Self Help – Abuse,

Keywords: Divorce, Teenage Independence, Interracial Interaction, Domestic Abuse, Family Instability, Basketball, Inspiration

First Printing: July 2021
21 22 23 24 25 26   10 9 8 7 6 5 4 3 2 1

Table of Contents

Introduction

Most of us will face some kind of challenge in our lives. In fact, I encourage you to think of one person you know--or have ever known--who has never had to deal with something unexpected, something that makes them feel hopeless, something that requires them to do something they really don't want to do, or something that makes them angry, sad, frustrated, or unsure about their own safety.

At least one of these situations happens to every one of us at some point in our lives. Often, we're left with confusion about where to go to find safety, or confidence, or even something as basic as peace. We aren't sure if anyone else is dealing with the same thing, which, of course, makes us feel like we're all alone in the world.

Those challenges we face come in diverse packages: big, small, life-changing, barely noticeable. They may be something as unique to us as losing a family pet, but they might just as easily be something as all-consuming as our family going hungry--again and again.

The more life forces us to focus on whatever challenges we face, the more we find ourselves unable to see or think about anything else. The challenges begin to control every waking part of our lives, many times even getting into our dreams.

In the story you're about to read, you'll meet a 12-year-old whose family is dealing with multiple major challenges. The family members face abuse, they face divorce, they face poverty and homelessness, rebellion, and much more.

It's only when the 12-year-old starts to see a much bigger purpose for his life, that he starts to see possibilities. For this young man, the purpose--and possibility--comes in the form of basketball. You see, life can work through almost anything, even a game, to help us identify what we might accomplish if we give our best to it.

This game ends up offering this young man a way to shift his focus from the crippling challenges his family faces, to a set of experiences that reveal an awful lot about himself, his family, and the world around him.

I hope this story helps you to see how you can find peace in the middle of the challenges you face. This can happen through just about any passion you have: digital design, gardening, artwork, running, puzzles. The list is limitless.

What shape the source of peace takes isn't what really matters. What matters is to find something that offers you the chance to build inner strength, a sense of self-worth, and most importantly, an awareness of how something bigger than ourselves works most meaningfully through you.

Find what passion is within you, commit time to it whenever possible, and watch for the lessons it teaches you. When that happens, you'll be that much closer to finding peace in the middle of those challenges you face, your very own calm in the storm.

Chapter 1

Basketball--A First Love

There's a beauty in seeing a child discover a passion. To see someone so young fall so completely in love with a healthy activity is to bear witness to a life being changed to an awakening of possibilities.

For 12-year-old Marcus Lambert, that passion arrived in the game of basketball. It reached into his life and took hold of every waking moment, every thought he had about who he was and what he wanted to accomplish. It became his best friend, his source of personal pride. It also became his escape: from the ugliness building around him, sure, but also his escape from the fear that he wasn't good enough.

It took him to places he had never been, places where life was different, better somehow, than anything he'd ever experienced. It took him to places where he was able to see a world with so much more than his own neighborhood, his own interests, and his own challenges.

When he looked at his life as part of this beautiful game, he had to admit that basketball became much more than his identity or where he went to find something bigger than himself. Basketball became the holder of his dreams.

"Bounce, bounce, bounce." The only sound he could hear was the ball coming off the floor, back to the softness of his hand. Again and again, bounce after bounce. More than 20,000 screaming fans and all Marcus Lambert could hear--and feel--was the ball and the court.

Four seconds left. Game six, NBA Finals, and Marcus had the ball exactly where it had always been: in his hand. He had dreamed of this moment for most of his life. IIis team had advanced through four playoff series, and now a championship was where it belonged: in his hand.

He crossed midcourt as the clock continued its count. Four seconds between now and an NBA title. Four seconds and his teammates, his coach, and the 20,000 fans in the arena trusted him to win it all.

Marcus took two more dribbles with his left hand, and then broke his defender's ankles with a crossover to the right. One more hard dribble, and he elevated just behind the arc. It was an open look at a "3" and as the clock hit one second, Marcus released the ball. The rotation was perfect and as he came back down to the floor, he could see the ball passing cleanly through the net, the horn sounding.

His teammates rushed from the bench, mobbing him, driving him to the floor. He didn't care. Nothing else mattered in this moment. All that registered was the crowd chanting his name. "Marcus, Marcus, Marcus." In the middle of the chaos, this made perfect sense.

Above all the noise, one voice caught his ear. He'd heard it before. Who was it? He knew that voice. Was that his mom in the crowd, yelling his name, celebrating with everyone else?

"How sweet is that?" he asked himself. His mom had seen him hit the most important shot of his life.

"Marcus!!" The voices continued. "Marcus. Marcus. Get up!"

"What??? What did she say?"

"Marcus, get out of bed. You're gonna be late, again."

"Are you kidding?" Was he dreaming?

"Yuck!" Was that drool on his cheek? No, someone must have spilled a drink during the celebration. It couldn't be a dream. Could it?

For starters, Marcus Lambert was only 12. While he loved the game of basketball, and in his mind, he thought he had some serious skills, he wasn't ready for the NBA Finals. He hadn't even finished 6th grade. He lived for this game, but anything bigger than hitting a winner from the far corner of the driveway would have to wait.

Marcus was the third of four children. He had a younger sister and two older siblings. His family lived outside of the city, where open fields in every direction fed his natural curiosity. His parents were hard-working people who expected their children to be the same, showing respect to everyone they met. It was a conviction formed through years of local church attendance. This was a family that looked to be built on integrity, but one whose reality often hid behind that appearance.

It wasn't easy for Marcus to connect with any one of his siblings. His older brother by four years was too smart, too impatient, and too focused outwardly to spend time building a relationship with his younger brother. His older brother's intensity often came across as anger and honestly, that frightened Marcus.

His older sister was only 14, but she had already left their shared childhood behind, instead moving in the direction of an active interest in boys; this usually led her to look for connections outside of her family. She had very little time--anymore-- and even less interest in hanging with her 12-year-old brother and his passion for dirt bikes and outdoor sports.

Marcus's third sibling, a younger sister only 10, had little interest in physical activity. That disconnect left what felt like no common ground for the two of them.

In the absence of anything meaningful with his siblings, basketball had become Marcus's best friend, and he spent every possible minute with it. When he got home from school each day, he'd immediately grab a quick snack and head to the driveway. He would shoot again and again. First from the left side, then from the right.

Every shot began with a hard crossover dribble from one hand to the shooting side, and then the elevation. Sometimes it was a short jumper, other times a drive to the rim for a strong finish. At least as strong a finish as a 5'8", 140 pound 12-year-old could muster.

Marcus had fallen in love with the sport less than a year ago. He remembered the first game he had ever watched: the Lakers were in Boston to play the Celtics. Perfect. West Coast style versus East Coast grit. The greatest basketball rivalry of all time.

The game came down to the last shot, which was also perfect. Lebron James took the jumper from the left corner, knockin' it down to give the Lakers a 2-point win. It was in that moment when basketball changed just about everything for Marcus.

He loved the competition of the game. He loved the skill sets basketball demanded. He loved the idea of a team coming together for something greater than self. He loved that the game let him escape from everything else. Most of all, he loved that the game offered chance after chance to bounce back from whatever just got the better of him. He had to admit it: there wasn't a single thing he didn't love about this game.

Chapter 2

This is My Neighborhood

Up to the moment he fell in love with basketball, Marcus had been totally content to ride his dirt bike in the fields surrounding his childhood home. Late afternoons after school, weekends, evenings until the day faded too far into night, Marcus was riding. He had become as comfortable in those fields with the grips in his hands as he was in his own backyard.

In fact, it was on that dirt bike where Marcus first experienced courage, and the challenge each of us face when trying to find it.

Directly across the street from his family's home, there was a drainage ditch, stretching the full depth of the open field, from the road to the larger canal at the back. The ditch was only three feet wide and equally deep, but when workers dug the drain, they left piles of dirt to the sides.

The older kids in the neighborhood took those piles and turned them into jumps--over the ditch. They'd ride their bikes over them; they'd eventually fly their dirt bikes over them too. They weren't huge jumps, no more than three feet high and 10 to 15 feet long, but they demanded some confidence to leave the ground and sail over the open spaces, and they inspired a desire to try in the younger riders, like Marcus.

Marcus rode in that field almost every day, and almost every day he would stop next to those jumps, wondering what it would feel like to sail over the open spaces to the other side.

What he really wondered was whether he had the courage to try. You see, most of us find courage in small steps. We consider, day after day, whether we'll be able to do something. Whether we have inside of us the willingness to take a chance.

Each of those days represents a small step in the direction of overcoming. For Marcus, this jump was no different. There was fear. There was a need to overcome that fear. And there was some instinctive desire to be free from that fear. After what felt like weeks of gut-checking, he found his answer: he was ready to try.

As the day arrived, Marcus rode his dirt bike to within 30 yards of the jump, just like he'd done almost every day for weeks. While it was only three feet tall, it was his giant, and he had to conquer it. He sat staring at the mound, like some boxer measuring his opponent. No one else was in the field; it was him and the jump. The isolation actually made it easier to focus.

After considering the obstacle one last time, Marcus found every bit of his courage. He let go of the clutch, turned the throttle, and accelerated.

Somewhere inside each of us is a "no turning back" button. Once we press it, we see ourselves as "all in" with whatever challenge we face.

Marcus had found and hit his button, and as he reached the pile of dirt, his mind was so locked into sailing over the jump that the idea of backing off didn't register.

Accelerating up the mound, Marcus felt his front tire leave the earth, followed quickly by the rear. It is in this moment, when we finally take the risk, breaking away from any hesitation that tries to hang onto us, that freedom from fear fills us. We have exploded through any barriers between us and overcoming.

Marcus was so focused on leaving the ground and landing safely on the other side that fear had completely lost its grip on him. All he felt was the adrenaline that came from trying.

Landing safely on the other side opened a new set of possibilities for Marcus. During the next hour, he repeated the jump no fewer than 15 times, each one a smooth landing on the other side. After weeks of wondering, Marcus's search for courage was complete.

Riding that bike, day after day, generated more than courage for Marcus. It created a sense of adventure within him, a spirit hungry to see. Straight across the street, down the road and to the right, behind the house. There were fields in almost every direction and every one of them offered another opportunity to explore his world.

Marcus's family had been in their new house for four years, but it was only 50 yards down the street from their old home, where Marcus was born. This was his neighborhood and with a dirt bike to take him, he knew every corner of it.

One afternoon led to one of the more important childhood experiences for Marcus.

The family that bought his first home had four children. The oldest was 15, a teenager who loved the "idea" of riding a motorcycle. The problem was he didn't have one of his own. Because of that, and because the families lived so close to each other, Marcus's dirt bike became priority number 1. Again and again, he asked Marcus if this was the day for the first ride.

Marcus wasn't sure how to answer the older neighbor; "He's in high school and I'm in sixth grade. What am I supposed to say?" he asked himself for the umpteenth time. It was a question without an answer--or at least it felt like it.

From somewhere inside, Marcus knew he'd have to let the neighbor ride the dirt-bike--sooner or later. What he didn't know was the experience that first ride would bring.

Marcus and his older sister, only 13 at the time, pulled out of the driveway and headed down the street for one of their favorite trails. Riding his dirt bike with her-- at least once in a while--was one of the few remaining connections with his older sister.

As they accelerated, their 15-year-old neighbor stepped into the road, waving at them to stop. Marcus pulled on the front brake and as the neighbor asked to ride, once again, Marcus knew in his gut this would be the day.

The bike was actually made for one, but with a slightly longer seat, it could handle two comfortably, if the riders were young enough. Neither Marcus or his sister wanted to step off and walk home. Using what felt like logic, they figured they could make this "three kids on a bike made for one" thing work.

The 15-year-old neighbor took the grips. That's what he wanted all along. Marcus's sister was in the middle, and Marcus was left with the sliver of seat in the back.

The three of them had ridden no more than 30 yards when they turned onto a gravel road, a familiar route to one of the neighborhood's favorite riding areas.

At the end of that gravel stretch, they reached a "T." Turn to the left, and they would head down a former tractor lane, now nothing more than dirt and grass side-by-side trails. Turn the other way, and they would pass a house on the right, then reach a gravel road with sizable potholes shaped through the region's annual rainstorms.

Instinctively, Marcus knew with three of them on the bike they needed to turn left and ride the softer trails. He'd been that way many times. It was definitely the better choice. Not only that, but the trails in that direction were also a lot more exciting. For whatever reason, the 15-year-old neighbor wanted the gravel road to the right.

The two of them went back and forth, with Marcus insisting they head to the left. Each time, the neighbor promised he'd be careful if they went the other way. After the third or fourth round of this, Marcus gave in.

"Okay, but we have to go slow," he said.

"I will. I totally will," the neighbor promised.

With that agreement, the kids took off, headed past the house on the right, and reached the potholes. It wasn't 10 feet before they hit the first dip, throwing all three of them from the bike and onto the rocks.

As Marcus looked back on the incident, his awareness of the neighborhood--and his bike--were confirmed through what happened. At only 12, he knew what he was talking about.

Marcus landed on his left side, his bike to the right, in the ditch. The older neighbor ended up behind him, with Marcus's sister Kristin just a few feet away.

Immediately, Marcus checked to see if his sister was okay. Somewhere inside of him he heard his parents' voices: "Check on your sister." After she confirmed she was okay, and the neighbor started apologizing, Marcus straightened himself and started to stand. No bones were broken but for some reason, he struggled to put weight on the left leg.

It was in that instant, as he fought for his balance and recognized something wasn't right, when he first saw the damage done to his left knee. To that point, any physical pain hadn't registered for Marcus. He was too focused on the wreck and his sister's safety.

But as he stood, he saw a gash on the top and outside of his leg, probably six inches, running up and down the knee. Actually, what Marcus saw in the middle of his torn flesh was his kneecap.

The only thing visible in that instant was white bone covered with smeared blood. His leg had been ripped open and it was then that Marcus realized how much pain he felt. He instinctively screamed for his sister to grab the bike and rush him home, where his mom would take him to the emergency room.

Looking back at that accident, Marcus realized this was probably one of the most remarkable things ever to happen to him. As a sixth-grade boy, gore was extremely high on the cool scale; Marcus's exposed kneecap was off the charts.

Very few people have the chance to see their own bone without an anesthetic--and live to talk about it. Marcus Lambert was now a member of what had to be some kind of select club.

This experience and many others were part of the foundation for life Marcus knew: a stable home; a familiar neighborhood; an intact family; a comfortable set of school experiences. At least that's how it all felt.

But all that stability for his young life was about to change, and like any other kid caught in their parents' separation, Marcus wasn't prepared for any of what followed.

Chapter 3

A Happy Home?
Not Remotely

Best he could remember, the arguing started sometime between his 11th and 12th birthdays. Every night, after Marcus crawled into bed, his parents would begin. It was almost like they'd scheduled the fights in advance.

Words like "jealous" and "unfaithful" repeated themselves, night after unsettling night. While he wasn't totally sure what they meant, he knew this much: those words were accusations, not descriptions.

"Will you two just stop it?" He wanted to scream at his parents, but an 11-year-old couldn't do that.

Lessons at church reinforced respect for parents. Talking to them like that was scary--and somewhere in his thinking, it felt like it might offend God. Instead, he'd wrap the pillow around his head and pretend it wasn't happening.

Marcus's father was a hard man. He worked hard, spending most evenings and weekends away from his family, providing more material comfort than they needed.

He practiced his religion hard, which is another way of saying he was more dictator than dad when it came to faith.

He also raised his four kids hard, taking a military-like approach to giving orders, and an inflexible expectation that those orders would be obeyed--immediately.

But the most damaging hardness showed up in how Marcus's dad treated Marcus's mom. Any hope she'd had of a marriage with compassion quickly left after they'd set up house. Her life, shaped by verbal abuse every day, became "his way or no way." Marcus's mom felt no softness from the man, on their anniversary, when they started arguing, or any other time.

It was a couple years earlier when Marcus had pushed back against his mom's authority. It's a 9-year old's way of testing his independence. He was challenging her position. His mother had reacted with discipline but within seconds, his dad charged into the bedroom with a 2 by 4 in his right hand, shaped into a paddle, grabbed his young son by the left arm, and started pounding.

Instinctively, Marcus yelled for his father to stop, but the pain of the blows took his breath away. He tried to resist but after the 2nd or 3rd strike, all his little body could do was curl into a ball and wait for the nightmare to end. That's all any child can do when an adult loses control. Discipline quickly became horror as his father's rage went unchecked.

Physical abuse of a child is always grossly one-sided, with the adult two or three times larger and stronger. Unless we've lived through it, we struggle to understand the terror a child experiences in the middle of a beating. All a child can do is hope to survive. The violence is so overwhelming, any controlled reaction isn't possible.

For close to two weeks afterward, Marcus felt the pain of his dad's explosion. His back and behind were discolored, the bruises were a daily reminder of how hard his father really was.

In most communities, his dad would be reported to the Child Protective Services, and then arrested, with Marcus entering foster care as a "ward of the state." In this family, and so many others with violent parents, children try to move forward, ignoring the nightmare as much as possible. In more dysfunctional homes, kids use the experience as part of some twisted defining of what parent/child relationships are supposed to look like.

All of his father's hardness crushed Marcus's mom. She was a sensitive woman who cared for others. It was her identity more than a description. She took care of her children; she took care of her aging parents; she was the answer when abused family members came running, bruises on their bodies, and faces swollen beyond recognition.

Marcus's mother cared. That was half his answer when teachers asked him to describe his parents. His dad was hard, and his mom cared. That statement captured everything there was to know about the woman. And dealing with her husband's hardness, year after year, ate away at all that beautiful compassion.

As the object of nightly accusations, the fuel behind all verbal abuse, some part of her was either going to die, or it was going to grow a crust of its own. The shell that formed would lead her to say "enough" before Marcus finished 6th grade.

Chapter 4

This Has to Change!

Every next morning was the same. Marcus's dad was off to work, and his mom had to forget the night before. She had to step into her purpose: Marcus and his siblings. They had lives to live and fights between their parents weren't part of those pictures. As much as possible, Marcus's mom held those images together.

Marcus's dad grew up the son of an equally hard man, a wealthy business owner and former military officer. All of that hardness from his own childhood prepared Marcus's dad for seeing only one way of communicating: his way.

Consumed by her husband's hardness, Marcus's mom headed toward her breaking point. She came from a conservative Midwestern family, where divorce simply didn't exist. All you ever heard--or needed to hear--was "til death do us part."

"Separation? Not part of our vocabulary. You marry, and you commit to it, for better or worse," she told herself, week after week.

She thought of her own parents' marriage. "They made it through an awful lot of ugliness. Am I supposed to do the same thing?" She cringed at the thought.

But when you deal with an abusive marriage long enough, you reach a point where all your thinking about right and wrong makes no sense. All you know is the de-valuing, day after painful day. You either become numb, or from some dormant place inside, some place that hasn't been nourished or fed for far too long, you become brave.

With the nightmare she was living always in the front of her mind, Marcus's mom chose bravery, and not just for herself. She asked herself again and again, "What am I doing to my kids if I stay in this marriage?"

That question, asked as many times as it takes, is what eventually leads many women to walk away. They can't allow their children to live within the nightmare any longer.

Abuse wasn't the reality she wanted for any of her children. "How will my sons treat women if all they see is their mom as some verbal punching bag?"

"How much confidence could my daughters hope for if the only model of a woman they see is their mom made to feel more worthless?" Those questions broke every bit of her heart.

With all of this working its way through her mind, she needed her and her children's lives to change. And while she would eventually find the courage to leave, another, bigger question remained: "How am I going to make this work?"

As a first step toward separation, Marcus's mom left town for the weekend with a girlfriend. She needed to find her courage and it wouldn't happen in the middle of the storm.

It was the first time in as long as she could remember not feeling buried under verbal assault. It renewed her soul and was the injection of strength she needed to move towards something better.

Within days after returning, his mom had made arrangements for Marcus and his siblings to leave their home, in the middle of the afternoon.

They would head down the street with the story that they were just taking a walk if anyone asked. They were to meet a man they didn't know, who would give them a ride to an unnamed family member's house. The details created a measure of suspense. With every step they took, the intensity grew, and the separation became more real.

In one of the more ironic moments of their leaving, the children's father came home from work early, in the family car, pulling up to the four kids as they walked along the roadside.

He wasn't an ignorant man. He must have sensed his family was coming apart; the pain in his face was obvious--and odd--to Marcus. He had never seen his father look vulnerable.

In his now 12-year-old mind he wondered what their leaving would do to his dad. It just wasn't something Marcus had considered: that his father, this hard, demanding man, would value the idea of his family sticking together. His dad had been the absent parent so many times, the harsh, unfeeling father, that the idea of his losing something when his children left didn't register.

Marcus's older brother, 16 at the time, took the lead.

"We're just going for a walk. We'll be back in a while."

Marcus wondered if his father bought any part of the story as he drove the remaining two blocks home. His father's life was about to unravel. As hard as he was, he wasn't ready for the emptiness that house would come to hold.

This is what "separation," the ultimate "S" word, does to families. It takes all that's familiar and tears it apart. There are definitely marriages that need to end--for safety if nothing else. And while kids are almost never the reason, separation always leaves them with the least to hang onto. This was as true for Marcus and his siblings as any other family.

Chapter 5

Not Our Life Anymore

"Where are we gonna live, mom?" "Does this mean we're not staying with our dad anymore?" "Do we have a home?" While the questions were sincere, what they really said was, "I'm scared. All I've ever known is gone. What's gonna happen now?"

These were some of the fears Marcus and his younger sister shared in the days following the separation. While they were staying at their grandparents' house for the time being, they knew it wouldn't last. They knew their grandma and grandpa were just trying to help.

In the middle of all the asking--and all the fear--what Marcus and his younger sister really wanted to know was, "What will our lives be like from now on?"

Their mom didn't have the answers they wanted. She had a million details to manage. She had to connect with a lawyer to file for divorce; she had to figure out how to pay for it; she had to find a place to live, which meant trying to figure out if there was rent assistance for her family. She had to visit the welfare office--again and again--to sign up for food stamps and medical cards. And so much more.

Because she hadn't finished high school, she had to find out how to sign up for a high school completion, and then consider what "career" she would pursue to help support her family. And all of this was happening while she was trying to hang onto some picture of faith. Daily she questioned where God was in the middle of her challenge. The answers would come, but not as she expected.

She made the decision to leave the marriage with as few possessions as possible. That meant no furniture, no ugly demands for a financial settlement, and only the family truck to drive. She would request child support, but that was it.

Her work ethic and pride would drive her to "do this on my own." It was easy to admire, but it didn't make their new lives any less challenging.

With so much pressure on her shoulders, it came as no surprise that she would question whether she could make it. Every detail she had to deal with was one more layer of doubt, one step closer to defeat. These were her burdens. She was the one who chose to leave her husband.

She was the one who said, "I can take care of my kids better without him."

The family had been members of a local worship community for years, something that could have helped so much during and after the separation.

But when Marcus's mom left her husband, there was a sort of "shunning" that took place. The community supported the man, while the woman and her children were now "outsiders." This family was no longer embraced.

So many worship communities aren't prepared for how to help families when divorce or death strikes. The changes in family dynamics are awkward, causing something uncomfortable instead of urgent.

This wasn't some ultra conservative branch of a faith where divorce was an unpardonable sin. But that didn't matter. The doors that were shut felt just as real. In the congregation's eyes, she was now living outside of what was acceptable, and she was taking her kids down with her.

What this family--and every family experiencing the same hardship--needed was compassion, not space to figure out the problems on their own. But that's what most people do: give space to those caught in divorce.

Ultimately, that "hands off" approach offers no help at all.

Consider for a minute how all this pressure impacted Marcus's mom's ability to connect with her children.

There were no "quiet moments" anymore, where she could just sit and be with her kids. No more trips to the park on summer afternoons, where they could relax in the sunshine, and the kids could play on the cool grass. There were no more patio chairs or sitting in the backyard with a cold glass of water, while the kids ran through the sprinkler.

All of that and so much more was gone, left behind at what used to be the family's home. From this point forward, life took on a much more basic requirement: making it through the next day. She was now a single mom, with four children and too many unanswered questions for how to provide for them.

Chapter 6

It's Not a Vacation

For Marcus and his siblings, summer used to be the best season of all. They'd go boating on the weekends. They would go to summer camps. They would play all day in the fields around their house. They would work part-time jobs, mowing neighbors' yards, or cleaning out sheds. Visiting their grandparents used to feel like a vacation.

Those days were gone. Instead, they looked ahead of them and saw a summer with very few possibilities.

"NOOO!! Why do I have to get up? School's out. How come I can't sleep in?"

Marcus had spent the last two nights on the hard floor in the living room at his grandparents' house, and now his grandma wanted him to get up and get moving-- to something.

His back was telling him this didn't feel like a vacation. It didn't even feel like a sleepover. It felt like a temporary . . . something.

He thought of his own bed, at his "father's" house. That still felt uncomfortable to say: "His father's house." Inside, he knew that everything from his past was gone.

They wouldn't be going back to their house, because "their house" didn't exist anymore. He wouldn't be riding his dirt-bike in the fields and on the trails around the neighborhood anymore because those fields were now in his past. And it wasn't even his dirt-bike anymore. He wouldn't be shooting baskets or attacking the rim in the driveway, because it wasn't his driveway anymore.

Everything he'd ever known was now not his anymore.

Marcus was only 12, but he was starting to realize what this "S" word, separation, meant. The life he knew, the home and neighborhood that were his world, were now just that: the life he knew.

What's a kid feel when his life is pulled out from under him? Is he able to think about what he's lost or about what that losing means?

Questions about where God is start to surface. Often, children from Christ-centered homes end up wandering away from their faith when faced with their parents' separation.

Other times, mothers are simply too overwhelmed to continue attending church, or making connections with worship community members. Their children's spiritual lives become the casualty.

Somewhere inside each child is this ability to recognize safe places. A place where it feels right to be.

When children are small and they hear some strange noise from the closet after the lights are off, they take their blanket, wrap it over their heads, and imagine it's a kind of force field, protecting them from anything unknown. Under that blanket is their safe place.

For Marcus and his siblings, their bedrooms, their backyard, the fields and their trails around the neighborhood, all these were safe places, and now they were gone.

His grandma was making breakfast--and noise--in the kitchen, and that snapped him back to the new reality.

What would he do today? What could he do? When you grow up with choices, you're able to see possibilities. That's because you have them in the first place. When you grow up without choices, it's hard to find "other things" to do. They've never been part of your life.

Today, Marcus was somewhere in the middle: he had grown up with possibilities, but because the life he knew two weeks ago didn't exist anymore, he wasn't sure what he could do, or what he should do.

He asked his grandma, "What's gonna happen to us now that we don't live with my dad anymore?"

She hesitated, mostly because she realized she was being asked to offer something stable, something like hope.

"Honey, your mom is doing all she can to make sure you kids will be safe. She's working really, really hard to find a place for you to live, to find a way to provide for you, and to make it so you don't have to be afraid."

"While I don't know what all of that looks like, I do know she loves you very much and she will do all she can to take care of you and your sisters and brother. It might feel confusing right now, but it will get better Marcus."

While Marcus wasn't sure about all his grandma was saying, just hearing her voice, the same voice that had taught him to read, helped him learn how to write, the same voice that had taught him to bake cookies and make pancakes, the same voice that had helped him learn about God, well, somehow it made his view of the world a little less frightening.

With breakfast finished, Marcus faced the same question as when he got out of bed: "What am I gonna do today?"

He remembered seeing a school down the road a few blocks from his grandparents', and he knew what that meant: Schools had playgrounds. Schools had open fields. Schools might even have other kids to hang out with.

He asked his grandma what the school was like and whether she thought he could go there. It didn't matter that he didn't have any ball or bat, or kite, or anything else. All that mattered was the chance to play something with someone.

"What will you do there Marcus?" she asked.

In her mind she was thinking about the older neighborhood kids and whether her grandson, at only 12, would fit in--or be safe.

"I don't know, Grandma, maybe play on the playground."

She knew what he was really asking. She knew he wanted something, anything, to do, as long as it didn't include sitting around a house with two "old people."

She also knew that if he stayed with her, her husband, Marcus's grandfather, would put him to work doing something outside.

While some work in the summer is good for kids, too much of it leads them to forget that they're still kids.

This whole "being with Grandma, just the two of us," was comforting to Marcus. His siblings were somewhere else in the house. He didn't know where and didn't really care. His grandma was focusing on him and nothing else. He hadn't had much of that lately.

Being a middle child and "easy to overlook" made it comfortable to get lost in playing ball or riding his dirt-bike. He felt like he mattered when he did those things.

He didn't have to hear anyone yelling. He didn't have to be told to keep his mouth shut. He could just ride, or just feel the ball coming off his hand for a shot or a hard dribble.

Because he couldn't ride anymore, and because he couldn't shoot in the driveway anymore, there was a pain inside of him when he thought about what he'd lost.

"I'm really gonna miss riding my dirt-bike," he realized out loud. His grandma could only stand and wonder what would happen to these kids.

"Grandma, I'm gonna go down to the school and take a look around and then I'll be back. Okay?"

For some reason, the school was sticking in his mind, someplace where he might be able to forget about what he didn't have anymore.

"Alright Marcus. I trust you to go straight to the school, spend a little time looking at what it has, and then come straight back here. When you get back, I expect a full report on what you found, okay? By the way, I love you young man."

With the sound of her voice in his ears, and the sweetness of her love in his heart, Marcus opened the back door and started down the street, hoping to forget what he had been forced to think about far too often.

Chapter 7

Playgrounds

Playgrounds are places with possibility. They are everything good about being a kid. They are pure play. They are where responsibilities and expectations go away. They are where the ugly things in children's lives disappear. They are where kids get to be exactly what they were made to be: kids.

And while playgrounds are these potentially beautiful trips into childhood, they are also places where important lessons are taught and learned, places where kids can challenge themselves and others, and places where children find out what kind of courage is inside them.

As a "veteran" grade school student, Marcus knew where the playgrounds were.

If you've got hundreds of kids out for recess or a PE class, you don't want strangers walking along the sidewalk in front of the school, with this unobstructed view of the students, or a clear look at which little ones wander off by themselves.

Location of play areas is one more layer of safety schools offer for children, and one more layer of reassurance they provide for parents.

As he walked around one side of the school, Marcus didn't see any of these playgrounds he was hoping for.

There was a chain strung between two steel poles, keeping would-be drivers from heading to the rear. Other than that, there was a parking lot, with no cars.

Like any kid, he was expecting to find slides, swings, cross bars. He had gotten his hopes up for something to distract him from his parents' separation.

What he found instead, as he kept walking toward the back, were open fields with backstops and goal posts, and outdoor courts with backboards and baskets fastened to brick walls. Not exactly the stuff to inspire a 12-year old's imagination.

In the middle of a growing disappointment, he hadn't realized that this wasn't a grade school, where 6 and 8-year-olds played outside during recess three times a day. It was a middle school, where 12 and 14-year-olds practiced what they thought it meant to be an adult.

Marcus didn't put it together at first that this was the kind of school he would become a part of in the fall.

He had finished 6th grade, at his neighborhood elementary school. The next step, of course, was middle school, with its tidal wave of bigger kids, each one rushing from one place to another, not paying attention to which smaller kid they slammed into on their way.

Middle schools were loud, intimidating places, where you had to find some courage if you wanted to survive. At least this is what his older brother and sister told him.

Was he the kind of kid who could find that courage, especially if he had no idea of what school would be his?

The whole idea of entering middle school was a little uncomfortable as he stood there looking at the large open spaces.

"How am I supposed to fit into a place like this?" Marcus asked himself out loud. That question was a gut-check for his confidence.

When kids are in the middle of their parents' divorces, one of the casualties is their self-belief. Because everything they've known as stable is now pulled out from under them, the last thing that comes naturally is confidence to face challenges--or changes.

Transitions happen for everyone but for children, they need something stable if they're going to pass through those shifts successfully.

Change is even more uncomfortable if a child is heading to a new school, one where they don't know anyone.

This is what Marcus was facing. Most children are able to transition from grade school to middle school with at least a few of their friends. They walk into a middle school together. They face those bigger, stronger, louder kids with each other, built through years of shared experiences.

For children experiencing their parents' separation, heading to an unfamiliar, new school is this extra layer of insecurity. It's this reminder of what they've lost, and of how much they're on their own. They don't know anyone, and everything familiar is now in their past.

Now that he stood face to face with one of these middle schools, he wasn't quite sure what to make of it. It was big, yeah. It was definitely a little scary. It absolutely was not a kid's playground.

He came to the school looking for crossbars and slides; what he found instead felt like some kind of test. He had an idea that the basketball courts he stood looking at, they were going to be places where he would have to prove something. Either to someone else--maybe someone older--or to himself.

Chapter 8

If I only. . .

"Grandma!" Marcus called as he walked in the back door. He was ready to report what he had found.

"Not so loud, Marcus. I can hear you just fine. I'm glad you made it back. Now, tell me what you found down at the school."

He loved how she wanted to know what he saw and what he thought.

"Well, first of all, I have to tell you it isn't a grade school at all. It's a middle school. I didn't even look at the sign in front when I walked up to the school. All I could see was the parking lot on the side, and it didn't have any cars. I thought 'Of course it's empty. It's summer break.'"

"What about the back of the school, where the playgrounds are?" She was genuinely interested in what he had to share.

What is it about grandparents that makes it so easy for them to listen? Is it that they've done most of their talking by this point in life, and now their energy levels like the idea of listening? Or is it that they have reached a point in life where they've done so much already, they are now eager to live life through their family members' experiences?

It's probably both those and more. Grandparents have a "seasoned" love that allows them to give all they have--including their attention--to those they love, and it was exactly what Marcus needed about now.

"Once I walked around the side and to the back, at first all I saw were fields with a backstop and soccer goalposts."

"It was pretty disappointing, until I looked to the left. That's when I saw the basketball courts. They weren't really courts, but you could definitely play there. They actually had baskets and backboards that were hanging on the brick walls of the back of the school."

She could see he wasn't quite sure about the potential for spending time there, but she kept prodding him to share.

"Did you see any other children at the school?"

"No, Grandma. That was one of the things that disappointed me. I really wanted to see some other kids."

"Marcus, it's still a little early in the day. It's not even noon yet. I bet if you go there in the afternoon instead of the morning, you'll run into some other kids. We definitely have children in the neighborhood."

She was working to keep his spirits up but couldn't have anticipated the next question.

"Grandma, I've really started to love basketball this last year. I don't know if I ever told you that. I'm wondering if you might be willing to help me get a basketball of my own. If I only had my own ball, I could go down to the school anytime, whether anybody was there or not, and play. I could dribble all I want. I could practice shooting for hours. I just love the game but I know my mom doesn't have any money for one, and, well, I don't know if I'm comfortable enough to ask my dad to help. He's never been interested in how much I like to play."

It was at that moment that Marcus's grandma realized the importance of an idea. She had seen the direction Marcus's older siblings were heading and she was sure they were in for some hard times ahead. As their grandparent, she could only do so much. Her heart broke every time she thought of what they might experience, but because of their ages, she had to keep her hands--and her words--to herself. They weren't kids any longer and her influence over them was limited.

She didn't want Marcus and his younger sister to see bad examples because they didn't have anything better to do. Not only would she buy her grandson a basketball, but she would also see if she could find other ways to keep her bright, curious--and potentially bored--12-year-old grandson from moving in the wrong direction.

Chapter 9

"Hoop" Dreams--Coming True?

The next morning, as Marcus got up from bed, again, from the living room floor at his grandparents', he had a little extra energy in his step.

He didn't know why, but he felt something like anticipation. What was he looking forward to? Was there something waiting for him and he just didn't know it yet? Whatever it was, it had him hurrying to go to the bathroom and get dressed.

Just like every other morning, Marcus's grandma was in the kitchen making breakfast. "Mornin' Grandma. How'd you sleep?"

"Pretty well young man. How did you sleep?"

"Well, my body is a little sore. I'm still not used to sleeping on the floor. But I guess I slept fine. I woke up feeling like something was gonna happen this morning. Does that ever happen to you?"

She smiled and gently said, "Oh yes. I can remember many times when I had some hope, or I was looking forward to something. I had a hard time falling asleep the night before and then when I thought about the next morning, it couldn't get there fast enough."

"Yeah, that's kinda how I feel this morning. Maybe it has something to do with the school down the road. I'm pretty excited about going to the school's basketball courts later today. Hopefully there will be some other kids there and maybe I'll get to play some ball with them."

"Marcus, I just can't wait any longer. Your grandpa and I made a decision yesterday afternoon. We decided that because you love basketball so much, and because you're now only three blocks from a playground, we wanted to make it so you could spend as much time there as you like, shooting all the baskets you can dream of. We bought you your own basketball Marcus. Let me get it for you."

It's funny how kids respond to dreams coming true. It doesn't matter if they're big or small, outrageous, or humble. The idea of anticipating something, especially for children who have very little, encourages them to see possibilities.

This may be one of the most important things extended family members can do for children dealing with divorce. Providing them with opportunity, even something small, like an ice cream treat, will keep alive their ability to dream.

Marcus was off-the-seat excited at his grandma's news. He asked just yesterday and now, his dream was coming true.

While his parents bought him a basketball before they separated, Marcus never realized how special it was. That's because when he lived at his dad's house, the basketball mattered, but it was only one of a lot of other things that mattered too.

"His dad's house."

"I wonder how long it will feel strange--and painful--to say that," Marcus thought to himself. The sense of loss continued to sting.

Here, at his grandparents', without any real idea of what home would look like in the future, having his own ball was all that mattered--at least in this moment.

Marcus didn't realize it at the time, but that simple gift of a basketball would become one of the most important influences of his young life.

That's often how life works: through small things or through people we may not expect to impact our lives.

His grandma brought the ball from some back room. It was in a big gift bag.

She handed it to him, saying, "This is to help your dreams come true Marcus."

And she meant it.

Actually, she couldn't have predicted how that one object would impact her grandson, but she certainly had every intention for it to be a difference-maker.

He quickly tore open the bag and there it was, a beautiful green and white outdoor basketball.

The new rubber surface let him grip the ball like it had always been part of his hand.

He started bouncing it in the dining room, not even thinking about whether that was okay. His excitement wouldn't allow him to stop.

His grandma watched for a minute and then, with the patience she always shared, said, "Marcus, let's eat some breakfast, and then you can go outside on the sidewalk and work on your dribbling, okay?"

"Thank you, thank you, thank you Grandma."

He just about jumped into her arms, but that would have knocked the older woman backwards. Instead, he hugged her for all he was worth.

He was now several inches taller than his grandma so when he wrapped his arms around her, his cheek rested against her forehead.

"You don't know how much this means to me. I was at the playground yesterday and having my own ball just seemed so far away. Now, one day later, I have it in my hands."

Chapter 10

First Lesson

Every ball player feels a little extra anticipation as they move closer to actually playing in a game. It's the adrenaline kicking in that makes the stomach a little tighter, or the imagination a little more unchecked.

That's true in every sport, but even more so when it's a game without a schedule.

That's what playground basketball is. No one knows who will be there. No one knows whether he or she will get to play right away, or whether they'll have to call "next," and wait for the first--or second, or third--game to finish before they get to step onto the court.

No one knows whether their team will win and get to stay on the court, or whether they'll get one game, lose, and have to sit down again.

Most of all, no one knows how well they'll play, what moves they'll make, and what kind of "game" their opponents will bring.

This is the beauty--and the unpredictability--of playground basketball. Every part of it is some kind of test.

That's true for older players, but even more so for younger players. Marcus was one of those younger players at only 12.

Just about anywhere he went, he would be younger than everyone else, which meant, of course, he would have a more intense education, and even more intense testing. His first trip to the middle school outdoor court would show what kind of student he was.

Marcus spent an hour that morning working on his "handle" along the sidewalk in front of his grandparents' house.

What he was really doing was honoring the talent he'd been given: the ability to play basketball. He was doing what anyone has the opportunity to do: give their very best to what they do well, with the desire to honor all who've invested in them.

We weren't designed to be mediocre. The idea of anyone telling a child that it's fine if they're just "ok" is ridiculous, especially when we're told that our lives have the potential for something more.

Inside every child is the possibility of the exceptional. The rest of us simply need to understand that excellence is about effort, not outcome. Not everyone wins a gold medal, but everyone can give their best to that pursuit.

With this conviction somewhere in the back of Marcus's thinking, he worked on pure crossovers, going from right hand to left, and then left hand to right. He worked on combination moves, sometimes going straight behind his back from left to right hand, followed quickly by an ankle-breaking crossover back to the left hand.

Every move he made was followed by a quick burst of two or three dribbles, just like he was exploding to the basket after beating his defender.

In the 10 months since he had officially "fallen in love" with the game, Marcus's ball handling had gone from acceptable to automatic. Anytime and anywhere the ball came off the floor, Marcus's hands were there, instinctively cradling it, ready for the next move.

From some on-line video he got the idea to dribble with his left hand--his non-dominant side--twice as much as his right. That meant if he was going to dribble 100 times with his right hand, in quick, close to the floor dribbles, he had to do the same thing 200 times with his left hand.

Because practice was pleasure for Marcus, his confidence with either hand was starting to make him feel like he could take just about anyone off the bounce.

After an hour in front of the house, Marcus went back inside. He gulped down a glass of water and looked at the clock.

"Almost noon. Players might start showing up at the playground pretty soon."

It was a half-hour and one peanut butter and jelly sandwich later when Marcus decided he had waited long enough.

Even if no one else was at the school, he would have his own ball and could shoot and dribble.

"How cool does that sound?" he asked himself. He had his own ball.

In a moment like this, with anticipation as your engine, it's easy to get impatient. Instead of sprinting to the school, however, Marcus took advantage of the three blocks walk and dribbled all the way. He was now one of those kids drivers-by see bouncing a ball along the sidewalk, headed to somewhere.

Marcus had learned to dribble back and forth between the legs as he walked forward and backward, around the back from either side, and to start his dribble with one hand and reverse pivot so he could spin off an imaginary defender, switching the dribble to the other hand as he completed the shift.

All of these moves and more, his "repertoire," showed up on the sidewalk between his grandparents' and the court, as he made his way to the school.

When he got to the school and walked around to the back, he didn't see any crowd of kids waiting to play baseball or soccer in the field, or lining the sides of the basketball court, watching for who the best players were.

Instead, he found two slightly older kids, shooting baskets with each other and talkin' a little smack.

"You think that's a jumper?" one said to the other. "Watch this."

The kid took the ball they were sharing and moved out to what would be the 3-point line, if there was one, and let go of a shot. It flew in a beautiful arc and found nothing but the inside of the rim, and the net below.

"Yeah, that's a sweet shot right there," the kid reminded his friend.

Marcus was impressed. These kids were a little older than he was, but they weren't a lot bigger. And they sure weren't gigantic high school kids. That made them a little less intimidating.

Because there were two rims attached to the brick wall, about 30 feet apart, Marcus went to the other.

He started with short jumpers, a couple from the left, and then a couple from the right. After he got a feel for how his new ball bounced off of the ground, and how his eyes saw the rim, he moved a little farther away.

He imagined a free throw line and started his routine. Two bounces. A 2-handed toss of the ball in front of him with a backward spin, so it hit the ground and bounced back to him. One more bounce, and a smooth release to the rim as his shooting motion held the follow through.

The ball hit the front of the rim, bounced against the backboard, and fell through the net. "Okay, I can shoot here," he thought.

He retrieved the ball and returned to the imaginary free throw line for a second shot. The same routine led to a clean shot through the rim and net this time.

Marcus was totally unaware of his audience: the two older kids.

After his second shot went through cleanly, one of them, the shooter, said, "Hey kid, nice touch. It looks like you've played some ball."

Marcus turned and with as much confidence as he could find said, "Yeah, I love this game."

"You wanna play a little 21?" the same older kid asked.

Marcus wasn't sure about the details of the game, but he wanted to play so badly he said, "Yeah, definitely."

That decision began Marcus's first playground basketball lesson.

"I'm Derrik," the first one said.

He was the one willing to talk smack with his friend.

"I'm Alejandro, but my boys call me AJ," the other said.

AJ continued, "We were students here. We just finished and we're both going into the ninth grade this fall."

Marcus introduced himself.

"I'm Marcus. My grandparents live down the road about three blocks. I'm going into seventh grade this fall, but I'm not sure where yet."

That was the best he could do on short notice. And the fact that Marcus didn't know where his family would live left him a little uncomfortable, and embarrassed.

The older boys didn't say anything. Maybe they understood something about Marcus's pain.

With the introductions out of the way, the boys got ready to play.

21 is a simple game and played when there are only three players, which isn't enough bodies for an even game of 2 against 2.

In "21" or 2-on-1, every player goes against the other two when he or she has the ball in her or his hands. When the ball's with someone else, the other two are on defense, both of them trying to stop the player with the ball from scoring.

The game has been called "Boston" or "Cutthroat" in many places, and probably other names in other places still.

If a player scores, she or he gets two free throws. Miss either one and the rebound is up for grabs. Make both, and the same player keeps the ball for another possession. The first player to reach 21 points ends up winning.

All of these details were new to Marcus, but as he didn't want to seem like he didn't know how to play the game, he didn't ask questions. That felt safer at this point. He also figured he'd learn as he went along.

The older kids said everyone would shoot to see who got the ball first. They called it "Shooting for outs."

Derrik stepped to the free throw line and made his first shot. AJ then stepped to the line and made his shot.

"Your shot next Marcus," AJ said.

Marcus stepped to the line, went through his pre-shot routine, let the ball go, and "thud." It missed the rim entirely and hit the brick wall to the left of the basket.

The two older kids looked at each other, looked back at Marcus, and almost smiled. But when they saw Marcus holding his head down, they didn't have the heart.

"It's alright," Derrik said. "We saw you over there. Relax. You'll find your game."

Because Marcus's miss eliminated him from the shoot-off, the two older kids continued to see who would get the ball first. After three shots, they were still tied. Neither one had missed from the free throw line.

They would have to start shooting from 3-point distance. AJ stepped back a few feet, grabbed the ball, and let it go. It was perfect, rippling the net as it went through cleanly.

"Alright, I see you," Derrik said.

"Check this." He let the shot go from the same spot as AJ.

As the shot headed to the rim, Marcus looked at Derrik's face. He was turning his head to one side just a little, biting his lower lip at the same time.

"NO!!!" he yelled, as the ball bounced off the back of the rim.

"I can make that shot anytime I want."

"Except for now, D," AJ countered, with half a laugh, and then followed up with, "My ball. You get to play defense boys."

While Derrik didn't mind talking while they played, AJ didn't say much. What AJ could do, however, was handle the ball.

As they started, Marcus did more watching than playing defense. That put him in position for the first play of the game. Actually, it put him "out of position."

You see, one thing he quickly picked up was that the player with the ball was supposed to look for which defender was easiest to beat, and then attack that side. In this case, it was Marcus, and AJ could see that right away.

AJ crossed Derrik over with a quick right to left dribble, saw Marcus standing there, and exploded past him to the rim on the left side. An easy finish led to free throws for AJ.

Derrik was quick to encourage--and challenge--Marcus.

"Just try to keep him from going to your outside. Instead, try to overplay him so he has to come back my way. I want you to be a thinker when you play D."

"That makes sense," Marcus thought.

"Overplay the guy with the ball so that you can get help from another player. First lesson learned."

AJ made his first free throw, but the second one bounced off of the rim to the left.

While Marcus was closest to the ball as it landed, he didn't go after it anywhere near as hard as the other two. Instead, Derrik beat both the others to the ball and started yappin'.

"Let's see what you guys got now."

Both defenders backed off just a little, so Derrik stopped his dribble and went up quickly for a jumper.

"Count that," he yelled, as the ball went cleanly through the net.

"That's 2 to 3 AJ," Derrik pronounced and stepped to the line for his free throws.

Marcus quickly realized two things: First, if he was gonna be able to compete with these older kids, he would have to play harder. The missed free throw showed him that.

They went after the ball harder. They focused on their opponent harder. And they seemed to believe in themselves harder than he did.

Marcus had never played a real game with others and so most of what he needed to know, he'd never had a chance to learn through game action. All he had ever done was shoot in the driveway, dribble wherever he could, and watch other people play.

The second thing Marcus realized was that confidence was gonna play a huge part in whether he could win or not--and not just today.

He watched Derrik and AJ and while they were different players, they both looked like they expected to play well.

"That's confidence," Marcus told himself.

"Let's see if I can put some of these lessons to work," Marcus thought.

Derrik squared himself at the line and let go of his first shot.

It was off the front of the rim and as it came down, Marcus stepped in for the rebound. He got the ball and instinctively started dribbling away from the two defenders.

"Ok, let's see what I can do," he said under his breath.

Marcus looked at the older kids. Derrik was inching toward him, while AJ stayed back just a little.

The court was open on his right side--if he could get past Derrik--so Marcus quickly crossed Derrik from the left hand to the right.

The older kid was standing up a little too straight and before he knew it, Marcus was by him on his open side, and pulling up for a jumper from about 14 feet out.

As Marcus watched the shot bounce around and drop through the rim, he yelled under his breath, "Yes!!!"

Marcus had officially scored his first basket against an actual defender. He had also passed his first test.

Marcus stepped to the free throw line for his shots. The first one dropped cleanly through the net.

He didn't realize it, but the confidence of beating Derrik off a crossover, and then knockin' down the jump shot, was showing up in how he shot free throws.

He bounced the ball for his second shot, spun it backwards so it came bouncing back to his hands, bent his knees, and let the ball go. Just like the first one, this one was clean through the net.

"Wow, believe it or not, I'm in the lead with four points!" he told himself, with more than a little excitement.

"Alright, alright," Derrick said.

"I see how this is gonna go. Marcus is gonna work us. AJ, we got to put a little more pressure on this ball player."

AJ bounced the ball back to Marcus. Immediately, both players came toward him, trapping him before he'd taken a dribble.

Instinctively, Marcus spun away from AJ, who was on his left side, hoping that would free him for a move to the right. But as he pivoted, Derrik anticipated the spin and easily knocked the ball away.

Derrik quickly recovered the loose ball and even more quickly attacked the rim off the dribble.

AJ went up with him, creating body contact as Derrik let go of the ball.

"Foul!" Derrik yelled.

"You got me man."

"The ball went in anyway D. You get your free throws," AJ countered.

"These guys know how to compete with each other, but they don't get mad," Marcus observed silently.

"Keep that lesson in mind too."

Derrik hit both his free throws, giving him six points to Marcus's 4, and AJ's 3.

As AJ checked the ball, he turned to Marcus and said, "Let's put a little pressure on him and see how he likes it."

With that, Marcus came within a foot of Derrik as AJ bounced the ball back to him.

Immediately, Derrik tried to accelerate around Marcus, who was already "overplaying to Derrik's left.

As Derrik realized he had no place to go, Marcus slapped the ball away and quickly recovered it.

Derrik and AJ backed off a little, allowing Marcus to pull up for a jumper, just beyond where the 3-point line should be.

It was a beautiful release with his shooting hand fully extended. Unfortunately, it bounced off the back of the rim, where AJ was already moving to rebound.

The three players ended up competing hard with each other for close to an hour. They played three games. Derrik won twice, AJ once.

Marcus managed to improve a little each game. By the end of the third game they'd played, he finished with 17 points, and made a lot of nice moves, jumpers, and finishes at the rim.

Even though he lost, Marcus felt good about what he'd been able to do against these older, stronger players.

He had worked up a serious sweat and had a chance to see what kind of basketball he could play.

"You can ball, Marcus," Derrik said, as all three players sat in the shade against the brick wall.

"You guys are bein' nice to me, and I appreciate it, but I've never played before. I'm sure there's a lot I can't or don't know how to do," Marcus responded.

"Doesn't matter," Derrik continued.

"I mean it kid. You've got some legit game. If you wanna keep playin' with us down here, we try to make it every weekday about the same time. If you want more than just 2-on-1, we'll try to bring some others. More players also come in the evenings. The school's got lights that come on at dark, and sometimes players go until 10 or 11. We don't usually make it that late. Too many family things goin' on in the evenings, ya know."

"Thanks guys. I really appreciate it, but I'm only 12, and I'm not sure my mom would be okay with me bein' down here after dark."

"That's cool," AJ shared.

"You can keep playin' with us during the day, if you want. I love the handle you have. You broke my ankles more than once. And when you started goin' after it harder, you played some serious ball. You are gonna be tough Marcus."

As he walked home, carrying his ball, Marcus couldn't stop smiling.

He thought about the last hour on the court. He had learned three important lessons about this game he loved. And if the older boys' words were true, inviting him to play again, he must have passed his first test on the court.

To anyone watching, Marcus was walking with just a little more confidence than even he realized.

He had taken the gift his grandma had given, a new basketball, and used it to find a place of confidence, where the ugliness of his parents' divorce had lost its power over him--at least for the time being.

Chapter 11

Applying the Lessons

Marcus was a kid who was more comfortable thinking about something than talking about it. That meant reflecting on his first time playing with AJ and Derrik as he walked to his grandparents' house.

That was the best thing he could remember happening in the last few weeks. Nobody arguing with someone else; nobody taking away something important. And nobody making him feel invisible.

"AJ and Derrik are only two years older than I am, but they made me feel like I belonged on the court with them," he thought.

"I love it!"

As he walked up the driveway to the back door, his attention abruptly shifted.

He heard someone yelling inside. Was that his older brother's voice?

Whatever it was, it brought him back to reality. He quickly remembered that he was in the middle of his parents' separation. He also remembered that his world had been turned upside down.

As he walked in the back door, he heard his older brother saying, in way too loud a voice, "You think you know what I was doing, but you really have no idea."

He was arguing with Marcus's mom, who sat on the couch, one hand over her mouth, head shaking slowly from side to side.

Marcus could see pain in her face, and he was immediately reminded of how much she had to deal with every day of this separation.

His older brother kept at it.

"The people I hang with make me feel like I belong somewhere. They don't treat me like I'm some stupid kid. And they give me opportunities for something better than this."

Marcus's older brother was one of the smartest people he'd ever known. He could take a problem without a solution, and in just a few seconds, process all of the details and figure out how to get past it.

It didn't matter if the problem was abstract, like how to get someone to agree with him, or something more concrete, like how to fix a damaged bicycle. His older brother had this ability to see how different parts needed to work together for something bigger or more important.

Unfortunately, and so many people have "another side" to them, Marcus's older brother was also one of the hardest people he'd ever met. He could say things to hurt others and act as though it didn't make any difference at all.

In this way, his brother was like their dad. He didn't seem to mind hurting someone else if it meant he got his way

Once, when Marcus was younger, he and his friends had been on the other end of the playground from his older brother and his friends.

The ball from Marcus's end had gotten away from the kids and rolled through the older brother's game at the other end.

As Marcus went after the ball, he went right through his older brother's game, instead of around it. 9-year-olds sometimes act without thinking.

Immediately, his older brother grabbed Marcus by the throat, not by the arm or shirt, but by the throat, pushed him against a nearby wall, and said, "Don't you ever get in the way of our game again."

Marcus responded, instinctively, with "I'm gonna tell Mom when we get home."

Their mother was a tall, strong woman, and each of her children would rather not cross her, even Marcus's 13-year-old brother.

On the slow walk home, Marcus's older brother stayed right behind, leaning forward and whispering, repeatedly, "You know what's gonna happen to you if you tell."

It was intimidation, pure and simple, and it worked. Marcus never told either one of his parents.

Years later, after he grew in size and confidence, Marcus would laugh about that incident. At the time, however, it reminded him of who his older brother was and how so much of what he did and said scared Marcus.

As Marcus listened to his older brother, now 16-years old, he realized, intuitively, that his family structure was about to change again.

He wasn't sure how, but he recognized in his brother's voice the sound of defiance. He was telling Marcus's mom that she had no control over what he chose to do. Every time she would start to say something, her oldest son would cut her off.

Marcus's mom, who had been raised with the idea of respect and compassion for others, and who had chosen at a young age to follow the beautiful life of Jesus, found it painful to listen to her oldest son.

His insensitivity was not what she'd hoped for. She couldn't have predicted the little boy she had loved, nurtured, and cuddled so many times, would become the defiant young man standing before her now.

Marcus's older brother, halfway through high school, was already showing some of the disrespectful, hurtful language that his father had shown to their mother for years.

This is the damaging impact that abusive language from one parent to another can have on their children. Those kids struggle to see the abused parent as an authority figure, someone to respect or listen to.

In all fairness, the abusive parent is also hard to respect. Each time they yell at, hit, or devalue their spouse or child, they are confirming the picture their children are forming of them: people who don't care about others or how much damage they do.

Marcus was now seeing signs of an abuser in how his older brother treated their mom.

Marcus was a sensitive and thoughtful kid. His concern was for his mother. Was there anything he could do to help her feel even just a little more peace?

Nothing came to his mind, so he went and sat next to her on the couch, and grabbed a hold of her arm.

"Mom, are you okay?" he asked.

By this time, his older brother had left the room--and his mom. Marcus could see she wasn't ok, but this was all he could think to say.

"No honey, I'm not," she replied.

"Your older brother thinks he doesn't want to stay with us as a family any longer. He thinks his friends will offer something better."

This was a little harsher than Marcus had imagined. He knew his older brother was hard, but this felt like it would break his mom's heart, and his brother didn't seem to care.

There had already been one "separation" for his family. Were they going to see another so soon? They only left their dad's house a couple weeks ago.

When older children experience their parents' divorce or separation, they often lash out, sometimes extremely. They feel betrayed--from their parents, from the lives they used to have, and for especially perceptive teenagers, betrayal from some "ideal" life they thought they were living.

Many adults suggest, often unfairly, high school is the time when young people sharpen their powers of cynicism. With the stability of life crashing around them, teens dealing with parental separation often begin to take an unhealthy view of life in general.

Issues like depression and pre-suicidal thoughts often work with this developing cynicism.

Instead of a hope founded in stability, they begin to doubt whether any good thing can come from what they're feeling.

This is also a time when teens may see some appeal to joining rebellious groups, or in experimenting with substances. For Marcus's older brother, both of these conditions were happening.

His brother had met and connected with some older kids whose lives were about defiance and drugs. And because of his older brother's intelligence, these older kids saw Marcus's brother as someone with value.

Marcus wasn't aware of his brother's details, but it still felt uncomfortable.

In the middle of this latest uncertainty, his thoughts went to what he'd learned earlier that day on the court with AJ and Derrik.

He had learned that you don't face an opponent alone. You look for help.

He had also learned you need to give more effort to something than anyone or anything else. If you don't, whatever or whoever you're facing will probably beat you.

And finally, he had learned you need to believe you are good enough to overcome something.

Every one of these lessons seemed to make sense in the context of what he was seeing now: a family falling apart. Those lessons also offered Marcus some strange comfort. Maybe he could use what he'd learned to help his mom in some way.

Chapter 12

What I Learned

Within five minutes after Marcus sat down next to his mom, his older brother was slamming the outside door behind him and heading to who knows where. He didn't say anything to her. He just left.

Another Prodigal Son breaking his parents' heart was playing out in front of Marcus and his mom.

He didn't understand all of the details, but for the first time in his life, he began to see the damage children can do to their parents, the pain they can cause through their decisions.

It broke Marcus's mom's heart and immediately she started sobbing, falling victim to the pain of her oldest child walking out of her life.

At only 12, Marcus wasn't quite sure what to do. His mom's body was shaking, she was slowly rocking back and forth, with this sound, almost like a wailing, coming from deep within her.

His mom's reaction frightened Marcus, but he knew he needed to do something, and physically comforting her made sense, so he just started rubbing her back.

He started from one shoulder and went to the other, and back where he began, and across again. Back and forth, back and forth, from one shoulder to the other. It's all he could think to do.

After a couple minutes, his mom started calming down, breathing more steadily, and actually sat up straight to look at Marcus.

Her eyes were puffy, and her cheeks wet, but she looked at him with a strong focus.

"Marcus, I know this will be hard for you to deal with, but I have to tell you that I don't think your brother will be coming back to live with us. He's really frustrated by the family breaking up, by the divorce, by not having a home to call his own, by a lot of things. And truthfully honey, I am so tired of fighting with him. It might look like I'm giving up on Jason, but I'm not. I will continue to reach out to him, and to be available for him whenever he's ready to talk. It's just that now isn't that time."

She continued, regaining control of her emotions. "So, I guess with your older brother leaving, in some ways, that makes it so you have to be the new 'man of the house.' This is a serious responsibility son. You think you're up for it?"

She sounded almost a little playful, but Marcus could also hear a lot of importance in the question.

"Mom, I will do whatever I can," he said, "but I'm not sure I know what a man of the house is supposed to do. I mean, do I have to go to work every day? Does it mean I get to make the rules?"

"Well honey, it means you help out wherever you can. If one of your sisters needs you to help move something, or help get supper ready, then you do it. And you do it with a good attitude."

"It also means you need to speak with kindness to everyone, even if you're in a bad mood. That's the example of Jesus, and it is so important if we're gonna stick together as a family."

"Being the man of the house also means you are ready to support someone in the family if they are having a rotten day. You just did that for me by rubbing my shoulders. That was exactly what I needed."

Marcus sat listening to his mom, amazed by how much she knew about being the man of the house. What she was saying was a lot different than what Marcus had seen in his own father, who really was the man of the house when they all lived together. In fact, most of what his mom was saying now was the exact opposite of what Marcus had seen in his father.

"Was that part of the reason she couldn't stay there anymore?" he asked himself.

"Mom must have learned an awful lot through her years of experience," he said quietly.

She was strong, even if she was crying hard a few minutes ago.

Her words also reminded him of how much he wanted to do things that would make her happy and make life easier for her.

"Grandma tells me you've been playing down at the middle school, Marcus. She said you told her you wanted a basketball, and she and Grandpa got one for you."

It was as much an invitation to share as anything, and the first time in quite a while Marcus's mom asked him about his life. It felt good to hear that from her.

"Well, yeah, Grandma gave me the ball earlier this morning and yeah, I played some ball down at the school today. That's where I was when you got here. Mom, I am so sorry if my being late to get back here made the argument between you and Jason worse than it coulda been."

"Honey," She was looking straight into his eyes.

Marcus also realized this was her reassuring voice. He remembered hearing this before, when Marcus had asked about where they were gonna live. He also remembered that voice from when his leg ripped open and he could see his kneecap.

"Whatever happened between your brother and me a few minutes ago had nothing to do with you,"

She continued. "He's got a lot of frustration he needs to work through. That will get better. I believe it. Right now, I just want to know about you and your day."

"Thanks Mom." That's all she needed to do: show interest in his day.

Parents have a remarkable ability to lift their children's spirits. Usually it happens through encouraging words, but it can just as easily happen by taking the time to meet a child where he or she is.

That "meeting your child" often looks like listening. Really, it's more than that. It's the most important person in a child's life communicating that the child matters more than anything else in that moment.

"I met a couple kids down at the school, AJ and Derrik. They asked me to play ball with them. They're going into 9th grade this fall, but I was able to play pretty well against them. They told me I had a sweet game and if I wanted to play more with them, I could show up just about any day at the same time and they'd be there playing."

"Actually, Mom, playing with these older kids made me feel a lot more confident than I've felt in a long time. I used to feel I could do a lot of things when I would ride my dirt bike, but once we left, and we didn't know what was gonna happen to us, I started to feel a lot less confident."

"Marcus," his mom was fully focused on him now.

"I know how hard this separation has been on you--and your siblings. I am so sorry for that. But you have to believe me when I say that as hard as it is now, it will get better. You will learn to fight against challenges, and you will learn how much strength is inside of you. That only happens when things are hard enough that we have to work to get through them."

"That makes sense Mom," Marcus quickly responded.

"The kids I played with today were really nice, but they didn't take it easy on me. At least I don't think they did. They showed me what I did wrong, told me it was cool when I did things right, and they made me work hard to do anything good against them."

"When I was walking back here to Grandma's house, I started thinking about playing ball with these guys. I learned so much and I'm wondering if some of it might help us as a family."

"It looks like you might have an excellent chance at making some really nice friends Marcus. Tell me about AJ and Derrik. What are they like?"

She may have been talking with Marcus, but she was really thinking about the kind of older kids Marcus's brother was getting involved with. She didn't want her 12-year-old finding unhealthy examples in older kids, so she had to know something about these two 14-year-olds.

"Mom, they were so nice to me. If I made a mistake, they told me to relax. They told me it was obvious I knew how to play ball. They made jokes but not about me, or about other kids."

"Well, I am thankful for that Marcus. It makes me feel better knowing you're meeting respectful kids. Tell me, what other things did you notice about how they talked?"

She knew that language was one of the strongest influences on children. If it was encouraging, kids were more likely to use the same kind of language with others, and feel better about themselves.

If the language was harsh, or mean sounding, or put others down, children were more likely to use the same kind of language, and that doesn't lead to being a person of character.

"One of the kids, Derrik, liked to talk a lot. He was always sayin' something. He said things like, 'Let's see what you got boys,' and 'I can score in so many different ways, you guys can't stop this.' But he never said any swear words, and he never put me or the other boy, AJ, down by anything he said. Oh, and when he would talk smack, he was always smiling."

"That sounds wonderful Marcus. I just want to know what kind of kids you're spending time with."

"Mom, Derrik was a little taller than me, maybe two or three inches. He's Black and was really quick with the ball."

"But more than the physical part, he seemed kinda like a teacher. The first time I played defense, I got beat pretty badly and the other kid scored easily. Derrik immediately stepped over to me, told me what I did wrong, what I needed to do differently, and even challenged me to think well on defense."

"You know, when he helped me learn something, he felt a little bit like an older brother. He actually told me to relax when he could see I was nervous."

At that remark, Marcus wondered if he had just insulted his real older brother.

Jason almost never showed any kindness to Marcus. Instead, he acted like he didn't have time to waste with a little brother.

Marcus knew Jason was smart, but he also knew how impatient he was.

"That's probably why he got mad at me so often, or why he didn't want to spend time with me," Marcus said to himself.

Marcus's mom could see his confusion and immediately reassured him.

"It's nice to have someone older looking out for you, isn't it? I bet Derrik has a younger brother or sister and knows just how to talk to them so they feel important. That's probably what made it easy for him to talk so nicely to you. I'm really happy to hear about Derrik, Marcus. He sounds like he might become an excellent friend."

With his mom's reassurance, Marcus continued sharing details about the older boys.

"AJ was maybe an inch or two taller than me and told me his real name was Alejandro, but his friends called him AJ."

"He didn't say much but I could tell he believed in himself a lot. Once, when Derrik was talking a lot, AJ kinda cut in and said something like, 'I don't think so, dude.' It was funny that he would get in Derrik's face a little, but it also felt like they were just two really good friends having fun with each other, and not afraid of hurting the other one's feelings."

Marcus just realized how much he had noticed about Derrik and AJ in only an hour or so of playing ball with them.

Marcus had friends from grade school he used to hang out with, before his parents separated, but this was different.

The kids from grade school were always a lot like Marcus. They grew up in the same neighborhood he did. They had been at the same school as Marcus for most of their grade school years. And they liked the same games on the playground as Marcus. Of course he would hang out with those kids. And, of course, he would know a lot about them.

But with Derrik and AJ, it was different. These were two older kids. They were definitely from a different school and probably a different neighborhood than Marcus. They weren't white, like he was.

They talked differently with each other than Marcus and his friends used to, like they were really comfortable with each other. They were also people he had never met before they asked him to play ball.

It made him wonder if maybe the reason they were so nice to him was because they liked basketball as much as he did. That was fine with him. He loved basketball and if the game made it possible to meet new kids, then that was great.

What Marcus didn't fully understand yet was how important it is for kids to have "common ground" with other kids. It's actually important for adults as well, but when you're a child, you don't automatically think of others as being like you or having the same dreams or interests as you have.

This "recognizing yourself in others" experience is huge for children as they move toward independence. It validates who they are. It reminds them that there's value in what they like and are drawn to.

For Marcus, basketball was becoming the vehicle that would provide a healthy path toward a positive self-image. And as Derrik and AJ were the first connections he made with the game, they became critical pieces for his journey, making possible Marcus's developing sense of self-worth.

"Mom, I learned three pretty important lessons from playing with those guys today. Would you like to hear what they are?"

"Yes I would Marcus. Can you wait just a second while I get a drink of water? I'll be right back."

As she came back into the living room, she sat next to Marcus and invited him to continue.

"Tell me what lessons you learned today while playing basketball Marcus."

He was pretty excited to share and hoped maybe the lessons would help his mom as well.

"The first lesson I learned came from the first time AJ had the ball. See, we were playing this game called 21. It's where one guy had the ball and had to play against the other two at the same time. Anyway, AJ beat Derrik with a crossover dribble and then got around me for an easy basket."

Marcus continued. "I wasn't sure what I was supposed to do, so Derrik put his hand on my shoulder and said, 'Try to play defense so that the other player has to come back my way.' That's called 'overplaying,' I think. It's where you play enough to one side so that the person with the ball has to go back to the other side."

"Anyway, what Derrik was really saying was to play so that I could always find help from my teammate. Don't you think that's a good lesson? I mean isn't it a good idea to always try to find help if you can't do something on your own?"

"That's a wonderful lesson Marcus."

Because she was someone who could guess what others were thinking, she had an idea of where her youngest son was going with this.

"Marcus, are you thinking there might be some way to take that lesson you learned, and see if it could help us find a place to live?"

"I hope so, Mom. I know you're feeling a lot of stress about a lot of things, and I'm just hoping there's someone who can help you solve some of those problems."

"Marcus, you are such a kind young man. I actually do have some people helping us. Maybe that will make things easier for all of us. In fact, your grandparents are helping us in huge ways, and not just by letting us stay here until we find our own home."

"Now, didn't you say you learned more than one lesson today? What else do you have to share?"

"Oh yeah. I did learn two more lessons."

Just knowing his mom really wanted to listen was exciting for Marcus, and she could hear it in his voice.

"The next lesson I learned was that if you want to win at a game, you have to play harder than everyone else. See, I was waiting for AJ to shoot his free throws. This is what you get to do if you score a basket. If you miss, everybody tries to get the rebound. If you make both your free throws, you get to keep the ball and try to score again."

"Anyway, I was standing on one side of the hoop, and Derrik was on the other, when AJ missed his second free throw. The ball bounced to my side, but Derrik got to it before I did because he went after it harder than I did. I realized right then that I needed to play a lot harder if I was gonna compete or win against these guys."

"Honey, that's such an important lesson. I have seen you work very hard at a lot of things. You worked hard at school and got good grades. You worked hard at becoming an excellent dirt-bike rider. You also worked hard at being an excellent friend. I want you to do the same thing with Derrik and AJ. I want you to work hard at being the best friend you can be to these older boys."

"This is what it means when we're told to love our neighbors. Be the best friend you can. You know what that means already. Now, don't be afraid to show them how important they are to you."

"Tell me about the third lesson you learned today Marcus. I bet it's going to be a good one."

Marcus's mom had this way about her that made him feel important.

"I bet she already knows this lesson," he thought.

"Well, Mom, the last lesson is to believe in yourself. When Derrik was talking so much and he would say things like 'You guys can't stop this,' it seems like he was really just showing how much he believed in himself. How much confidence he had."

"You know, when I started believing I could play with these older guys, that's when I started scoring or getting rebounds, or maybe tipping away the ball from one of them. It's amazing how much believing in myself helped."

"Marcus, you are going to find that confidence is one of the greatest gifts anyone will ever have. Even if someone older does something hurtful to you, or if someone tries to make you feel stupid or like you can't do something, you have to believe that who you are and what you can do are important, and no one can take that away from you if you know it's true. We weren't meant to be afraid, or to run away from challenges. We have the ability inside us to overcome."

"I love you so much Marcus. I just want so many good things to happen for you."

Even though his older brother had broken his mom's heart by leaving, and even though he saw her break down and cry, Marcus felt like this had been a really important day for him, at the playground and sitting on the couch with his mom. Every child needs positive examples, even as they become young adults.

Listening to his mom talk and knowing how much she wanted to hear what he had to say, made him realize that the most important example he could find of the kind of person he wanted to become, was right in front of him.

It was his mom, and as his family would face many challenges in the weeks, months, and years to come, her example as a person with strong character would carry him much further than he could imagine.

Chapter 13

What She Found

It was late afternoon and with Marcus's older brother now gone from his grandparents' house, Marcus's mom needed to clean out the bedroom where Jason had been staying.

Like many 16-year-olds, Jason did not keep the cleanest room. There were papers on the bed and floor, the sheet he had slept under was twisted and hanging halfway off the bed. The little dresser where he kept his clothes had drawers partially open, with a few left-behind items hanging half in and half out.

Each item she picked up seemed to remind her of her oldest child, and the little boy he once was. Only 16, and he was already gone from her home, her life, her protection and maybe from her influence.

"Home. What does that word look like anymore?" she asked herself.

When the pain is deep, it's hard to keep hopelessness away. Every picture of the one lost is a piercing reminder of what you can't hold onto. Every smell brings back some connection with what you used to have.

As she picked up the scattered items, she opened drawers, stuffing more into each one than it was meant to hold.

She opened the fourth drawer when she saw what she hadn't thought to imagine: a small plastic bag with 8-10 blue, round-shaped pills.

She picked up the container, opened it, and pulled out one of the items.

"Oh, please have a brand name," she told herself, hoping for what she knew, in her soul, couldn't be true. These were not prescription or over-the-counter pills.

Feeling unstable, she left the bedroom and sat down at the dining room table, opened her laptop, and started searching for images.

Typing in "illegal pills," she hit "return" and waited for the images to appear. Yellow pills, pink pills, white pills, red pills, and blue.

She immediately saw on her screen what she was holding in her hand: an opioid-based product, potentially laced with Fentanyl, a terribly dangerous substance, and used as a sedative.

She knew what could happen when people combined sedatives with alcohol. Their chances of overdosing skyrocketed.

The thought of her oldest child getting caught up in this was more than she could take. She leaned to one side and fell to her knees, scattering the pills on the table and floor. Screaming followed quickly, for what was happening to her family. Curling into a ball on her side on the floor, rocking back and forth, Marcus's mother's crying intensified.

Marcus's grandmother, his mom's mom, was there in an instant, on the ground and wrapping her arms around her daughter.

At the same time, she was calling for her husband, Marcus's grandpa, to get the keys. They would take their child away for now. She did not want her grandchildren to see their mother like this.

Within two minutes, Marcus's mom and grandparents were out the door, in the car, and on their way to somewhere else.

Marcus, his younger sister Maddie, and their older sister Kristin stood staring at one another in the dining room doorway.

Marcus's grandma had thought to close the laptop and quickly pick up the pills left on the table and floor. Those were not images or items to leave for younger children.

Maddie, only 10, asked, "What are we supposed to do now? All the grown-ups are gone." She knew as long as an important adult was present, the children were safe. As soon as that security ended, whether it was for an hour or a weekend, her world started shaking.

Kristin, who was 14, and having already experienced a bit more of life than she should, was quick to respond.

"I'm here with you guys. We will be okay. Grandma and Grandpa will take good care of Mom. For now, we can watch something on TV."

It wasn't the most comforting thing the younger kids would hear that day, but for now, it would have to do.

Marcus and Maddie sat on the couch in the living room while some show started.

Instead of grabbing their attention, the children quickly realized Kristin had already left the room. She had her own space at their grandparents' house, and they could hear through the door that she was talking with someone on her phone.

Marcus was curious, so he slipped over to the door and listened to his sister's voice. "Yeah, I would love to meet you later tonight. For now, I have to watch my little brother and sister. I don't know how long but I'll message you when I'm free."

After a pause, she continued.

"Definitely, I can only take so much of this mess. I wanna be with you more than anything else right now."

"Great," Marcus thought to himself. "Now my older sister wants to leave too."

Immediately he started thinking about his mom--again.

"How much of this can she take? How much of this can our family take?" He asked himself.

Kristin wanting to get out felt a lot like the next family fracture waiting to happen, and after what he saw his mom deal with today, it might not be the last one.

Chapter 14

Recognizing the Escape

The rest of the evening was a blur for Marcus. He remembered his grandma's neighbor coming over and making dinner. He remembered getting ready for bed by himself. He remembered the house being too quiet. He also remembered not seeing his mom the rest of the night. Any other details kind of fell to the side.

"I know we're kids, but shouldn't we know something about our mom?"

The question remained in his mind, not his mouth. Asking about his mom didn't seem right after what he saw that afternoon, but he couldn't let it go. He cared too much about her. Maybe tomorrow would bring some answers.

Lying in bed, with the quiet all around him, his mind went back to how good it felt to play ball with AJ and Derrik earlier that day.

"Was it really just earlier today?" he wondered.

"Is that possible?"

So much had happened, and he had seen so much of his family falling apart, it felt like that first game was days ago, not just a few hours.

He lay in bed, thinking about playing. And as he replayed each move he made, each shot he knocked down, he began to realize that basketball was just about the opposite of what being with his family felt like.

Maybe comparing his family's challenges with basketball wasn't fair. Hadn't he loved seeing how much his mom wanted to hear about his day? Hadn't she asked him to be "the man of the house"? Those were definitely cool.

But at the same time, hadn't today brought a ton of pain to Marcus's family? In that way, basketball was definitely the opposite. All basketball offered was excitement and a chance to prove something--to others and to yourself.

Lying on the floor in the living room, ready to drift into sleep, all he could think about was tomorrow, and the chance to escape; the chance to play some more ball down at the middle school.

Marcus slept in bits and pieces. This happens for many children when they realize their parents are dealing with serious challenges.

Kids are naturally more sensitive or attuned to family members' pain than adults. It's because so much of a child's well-being comes from how stable their parents' lives are.

In Marcus's case, he had two points of focus coming from this day, and both of them made it hard to sleep: One, his mom had gone through a terrible day.

His mom had her heart broken more than once, and to finish it, she had a total meltdown. When she found out it was also in front of her kids, that would probably make it even worse for her.

What Marcus only partially realized was that he also had a hard time sleeping because of his anticipation for playing basketball the next day. Anticipation uses adrenaline to keep our focus sharp.

Marcus couldn't stop thinking about what he hoped to do when he played again. He thought about moves he would make, about whether any new players would come, and what lessons he would learn from his second day on the courts.

As he restlessly drifted off to sleep, he could only imagine what it would feel like to compete---and escape--again.

Chapter 15

Sticking Together

The next morning started like most days for Marcus, with one exception: he had never felt this much anticipation. He remembered looking forward to a lot of different things in his young life, but because of how hard it was to watch his older brother and mom yesterday, the idea of playing ball today was different.

The anticipation he felt now was more than a "bounce in his step." This was something like a deep hunger or thirst for something you don't automatically have. That's what basketball had become for Marcus: something like a medicine.

His crumbling family was the illness, and basketball was the prescription. Maybe that picture was unfair to his family, but it's sure what it felt like to his 12-year-old thinking.

When kids are faced with multiple family crises, all happening at the same time, they simply don't have the skill sets or life experiences to figure out how to manage what's in front of them. Instead, they make sense out of the confusion through something they know. For Marcus, that was playing basketball.

The ACEs study began looking at the impact of childhood trauma on a young person's ability to function well, close to 20 years ago. The study examines single and multiple-trauma impact, and identifies areas where children are likely to struggle to function positively because of that impact.

Every person interested in advocating for children dealing with family instability should become familiar with the study's findings and insight.

For Marcus and his siblings, they were in the middle of significant, multiple traumas, a lot of it happening within the last 24 hours. Whether Marcus fully understood it or not, basketball was his coping device. It was his way of making sense of the confusion all around him.

In truth, basketball was much more than a coping device for Marcus. Playing basketball was one of the most important talents Marcus had been given, and it was the most important tool available right now to help Marcus make sense of the pain he was experiencing. The game gave him the chance to step away from the impact of trauma, while at the same time feed his passion.

It was already mid-morning when Marcus made it to the kitchen for breakfast.

As always, his grandma was there with pancakes. Because he loved them, and because he loved being with his grandma, Marcus could feel his mouth watering as he grabbed a plate, slathered on the peanut butter, and let the syrup drizzle.

"Marcus, I need to know how you're feeling this morning," his grandma asked.

She was a caring woman, just like Marcus's mom, but she also knew how to "get to the point." She was doing that right now. She wanted to know how yesterday's events had impacted her grandson.

"Well, it was pretty hard watching my mom go through so much yesterday. Jason tells her he doesn't want to be part of the family, and right after that, she finds pills in his drawer, and everything falls apart. I don't know what I'm supposed to do. All I want is to take her pain away, but I don't know how to do that. I'm only 12."

His grandmother could only stare in wonder at this young man, shaking her head slowly from side to side, while moisture formed in the corners of her eyes.

"Marcus, you have such a good heart. And because of that, I want to share just a little with you about how your mom's doing."

"Your grandpa and I took your mom for a drive yesterday, a really long drive, but it was what she needed to feel like she could face today. We actually went all the way to the coast, had dinner there, and then made it back late last night, after you kids were already asleep. That's why our next-door neighbor came over for a few hours. We called her and asked her to make dinner and sit with you kids until we got home."

"Your mother is carrying such a heavy load right now, with the divorce, her family falling apart, her wanting to protect you and your younger sister, especially, from all that's going on. She really just needed to step away from all of it for a while. Your grandpa and I were able to make that happen for her. This morning, before she left, I could already see she felt much better about facing whatever happens today."

"You know Marcus, when your mom was a little younger than you, maybe Maddie's age, she used to do her best to take care of everyone else. If there was a cat that had gotten into a fight with a raccoon, your mom was the first one to help. If I was in any kind of pain during the day, your mom was the first of my children to take over my chores. This is who she is."

"She cares deeply and because of that, she hurts deeply when things aren't right, like yesterday. But today, she's stronger. Remember this lesson whenever you're wondering how you can help your mom. Try to give her a chance to step away from all that bothers her, even if it's just for a short while."

"Grandma, I have been thinking about the same kind of thing, getting away for a while. Only with me, it's not a ride in the car or a trip to the coast. It's a trip to the basketball court that helps me forget about what's going on with our family. Basketball makes me feel like everything can be ok again, like it's gonna be alright if I can just get on the court."

"Well Marcus, it sounds like you have found a little bit of an answer. You are way ahead of a lot of people. And because you have found your peaceful place, we need to make sure you get as much time to play today as possible. Let's get you a good breakfast. I want you to help me with a couple things around the house, and then it'll be about time for you to head to the school down the street."

Once again, spending time talking with and listening to his grandma made it so Marcus could see much more clearly how to handle life. She always seemed to know exactly what to say to make Marcus feel like things were going to get better.

Feeling much better about his mom and the day, he sat down and started on those delicious pancakes. With each bite, his mind drifted a little more in the direction of basketball.

Chapter 16

Advanced Studies
(The Next Day at the Courts)

Marcus's trip to the playground after breakfast and helping his grandma was a lot like yesterday. He had a serious "bounce" to his step as he dribbled his ball down the sidewalk.

"I could do this every day and never get tired of it," he thought, as he worked on crossover dribbles, spin moves, hesitations followed by bursts, and between the leg combinations.

Just dribbling filled him with confidence. He realized after playing ball yesterday that there was a lot more to the game than just a great handle, but with the ball bouncing right back to his hand, every time, no matter what dribble move he used or where it came off the sidewalk, his self-belief felt like it was on solid ground again.

As Marcus approached the school, he thought he could hear voices coming from the back.

"That's funny, AJ and Derrik weren't this noisy yesterday," he thought.

What he couldn't have predicted--or anticipated--was that it wouldn't be just a game of "21" today. There were more players who joined the two from yesterday. Today, Marcus's education on the court would take on an advanced level.

"Hey Marcus, it's about time you showed up." Marcus knew that voice already: Derrik.

"Hey Derrik, it's good to see you guys. I was hopin' you'd be here today. I can't tell you how much I loved playin' with you guys yesterday."

Marcus's appreciation was touching to the older kids. "Are you kiddin' Marcus?" AJ jumped right in, making Marcus feel welcome.

"We loved ballin' with you too. Remember, you have a sweet game dude."

This might be the most Marcus had heard AJ talk. No matter, it was great to see these guys.

"Hey, we wanted to play more than 2-on-1, so we brought three more with us. We got 3-on-3 today!" Derrik said.

Marcus could hear the energy in Derrik's voice.

"Let me introduce you guys. Marcus, these are our classmates and AAU tournament teammates. Valerie is a serious baller. Her families from Vietnam and she's been playin' ball with AJ and me for a little more than a year now. Kenny lives down the street from me. We been ballin' together since kindergarten. Actually, we just shot in his driveway at that point, but you gotta start somewhere. And finally, this is 'Big Man Miles.' He is the dominator--when he plays like he means it."

"So, you guys," Derrik continued, "Marcus is startin' 7th grade in the fall, but AJ and I met him yesterday right here. We played some "21" and after close to an hour, we saw this kid has some tight game. We wanted the three of you to have a chance to play with him too."

Marcus couldn't help checking out the new players. He was now right around 5'9" and almost 145 lbs. Valerie must have been about the same height as him, maybe an inch or two shorter, but she actually looked a little stronger.

Kenny was at least the same height as Derrik, maybe 5'11", or just a little taller. And Miles, well, he looked like he could easily be over 6' tall. Marcus had never played ball with anyone as tall as Miles, so he couldn't tell for sure.

"Great to meet you guys. AJ and Derrik let me play ball with them yesterday. It was the first time I ever did anything more with the ball than dribble on the sidewalk or shoot in my dad's driveway."

He wondered if he should have said anything about not being at his dad's anymore. "Maybe they won't care. Maybe they know somebody else whose parents are divorcing too," he tried to reassure himself.

"Hey, it's all good," Kenny said. "We got your back if somethin' doesn't work real well out here. We love the game, but we also love to help younger players with their skills. We got you ok?"

"Thanks a lot," Marcus said in response.

"Can you believe this?" he asked himself.

"These older kids are unreal. They actually want to help me improve."

As he put his water bottle off to the side, he could feel the same tightness in his gut that he felt yesterday, when he stepped to the line for his shot during the shoot-off.

Just like yesterday, Marcus was the youngest player on the court. Because of that, it felt like he was going to have to prove something--again. He knew he'd have to prove to himself that he could play with these older kids. It felt like they'd be patient with him, but he couldn't know for sure.

"You can do this Marcus," he kept telling himself.

He would definitely be the skinniest player on the court. That probably meant he wouldn't be as strong as anyone else on the court.

And because they weren't playing "21" anymore, he knew he was going to have to learn more about the game and do it quickly. Otherwise, he wouldn't last even 10 minutes with these older kids.

"So Marcus, we're playin' 3-on-3 today." Derrik took the lead on introducing the game. "That means we have 3 players on each side. I'm gonna have you and AJ with me to start. We'll see how that goes."

"One of the things you have to know how to do," Derrik continued, "is learn how to switch on defense, and how to use your screens really well."

Marcus's mind was already trying to figure out what screens and switching were. The switching made sense. It sounds like you just switch to another player. What he wasn't sure of was why you would switch, or when.

The screens--Marcus wasn't sure about what those were. That's one of the things he would have to figure out on his own.

"Let's shoot for outs," AJ announced.

"I'll shoot for us. Who's up for you guys?"

"I'll shoot." It was Valerie.

"You first," AJ said.

With that word, Valerie stepped to where the 3-point line would be, tossed the ball in front of her and let its backwards spin bring the ball right back. At the instant she caught it, she went up for a beautiful jump shot. It caught the inside of the front of the rim and dropped through cleanly.

"Let's see what you got, AJ" she said, smiling confidently.

"Been workin' on your release, or you gonna throw up somethin' weak?"

She was having fun with AJ, trying to get him to laugh, maybe make it a little harder to concentrate.

"Watch this V."

AJ tossed the ball in front of him, just like Valerie had, caught the ball and went up. The ball hit the left side of the rim, bounced straight back to the backboard, and rolled off the front of the basket.

"That did not feel good comin' off my hand," he said.

"Maybe a little more work on your J?" Valerie asked--innocently.

"Yeah, thanks coach," AJ countered.

They were having fun talkin' some smack with each other."

"Alright, you guys get the ball first. First to 15," AJ announced. "Loser's outs."

So much of what these guys were saying sounded like a foreign language to Marcus. "First to 15?" "Loser's outs?" "What are they talkin' about?" he asked himself. He knew he'd figure it out, eventually, but he felt a little lost in the meantime.

"Marcus, you guard Valerie. AJ, you got Kenny. I'll play Miles," Derrik announced.

Every one of these guys spoke with so much confidence. Everything they said showed how much they knew about this game.

"I want to get to that point," Marcus told himself.

For now, he needed to learn quickly, or he had a feeling he might get blown off the court.

"All right Marcus, check ball," Valerie said as she bounced Marcus the ball.

He caught it but wasn't quite sure what "check ball" meant, so he held the ball in his hand, looking at her and back to the ball, while the others stood waiting.

Valerie could see Marcus's confusion, so she volunteered the info he needed.

"Marcus, 'check ball' means I pass the ball to you and you check to make sure your teammates are ready to play defense before you give me the ball back."

"That makes sense," Marcus replied.

"Thanks for helping me with that."

He checked to see if AJ and Derrik were ready. They offered quick head nods, and Marcus bounced the ball back to Valerie.

The game started quickly enough with Valerie passing to her right side where Kenny was. She immediately went to set a screen on AJ, who was playing defense and yelling "Switch on the screen."

Marcus now knew what a screen was. It was where one player blocks a defender with his or her body, so their teammate can maybe get free for a shot.

AJ continued yelling "SWITCH, SWITCH" to Marcus, as Kenny came off the screen with the ball.

Marcus was smart enough, or quick enough to figure out he needed to now guard Kenny as he came toward him with the ball in his left hand.

Kenny, who wasn't shy about attacking the rim, immediately put on a burst of speed, blowing by Marcus to the rim and scoring the left-handed layup.

Marcus immediately thought of how AJ got by him so easily as they started playing yesterday.

"What do I need to do to be more ready to stay between the guy I'm guarding and the basket?"

He wasn't sure, but he wondered if maybe not standing up so straight would make it easier for him to move more quickly.

"Lesson 1," Marcus told himself.

"If the player I'm guarding is going to set a screen for someone else, I need to see that ahead of time and plan to switch before my teammate yells. That should also help me to be in better position to play defense when I do have to switch."

Actually, the bigger lesson he was learning was that he needed to be more aware, earlier, of what was going on around him.

"Ok, ok," Derrik said.

"Marcus be sure you're ready to play "D" when that player comes off the screen. We don't want anybody gettin' to the rim for easy buckets. Our coach tells us to get down in a defensive crouch. That means to bend your knees a little. Yeah, like that, and then be ready to move as quick as you can, side to side. Try that."

Marcus nodded, bent his knees, and slid to one side, then back the other way.

Kenny chimed in.

"If you're slidin' like you should, you should be on your toes just a little, and able to move more quickly than standin' straight up. Our coach actually calls this a "slide drill," and we do it for hours at some practices. Least it seems like hours. He says, 'keep your hands up, and your butt down.' I think he just likes to see us in a little pain now and then.``

Marcus understood if he was gonna play with these guys, he would have to learn a lot, and do it in a hurry. He had ball-handling skills. It was the defense where he wasn't especially confident yet.

"Your ball D," Valerie said.

She wanted to help Marcus a little, so she shared what "Losers' outs" meant.

"Marcus, when we're on the playground, we play winners' outs or losers' outs. Winners means if you hit a basket, you get to keep the ball until you miss or the other team turns you over. If it's losers' outs, that means if you score, the other team gets the next possession. That's why you guys get the ball now, cause Kenny just scored."

Derrik stepped to the top of what would have been the key area. Miles was guarding him so Derrik had Miles check the ball. When Derrik got the ball back, he motioned for Marcus to come get the ball.

Marcus was on Derrik's left and actually had to fight through Valerie's contact as she was playing physical defense.

She wasn't grabbing his shirt or pushing on him. She just anticipated where he was gonna go and got to the spot quicker than he did. That meant he ran into her, which made him have to kinda fight through her physical contact to get to the ball.

Marcus came around Derrik as the older player turned his back to Miles, setting a screen on Valerie at the same time as Marcus took the handoff. Miles, all 6' plus of him, now switched onto Marcus, who wasn't quite sure what to do.

Somewhere in his thoughts, Marcus sensed he might be quicker than the taller player. With that, Marcus's ball handling helped him explode past the taller player to the right, staying low enough that Miles couldn't put a hand on him as he drove toward the basket.

As Marcus passed Miles, Kenny, who was guarding AJ on the right side, stepped over to help, shifting right into Marcus's path. That move forced Marcus to pass or kick the ball to AJ on the right, who was wide open for a jumper from about 18 feet away.

"Sweet pass Marcus," AJ was yelling, after he hit the shot.

"2 apiece everyone," Derrik chimed in.

Marcus had just learned his next lesson: If someone gets in your way, you don't have to be the one who scores or solves the problem. Don't be afraid to let someone else provide the answer.

The pass to AJ for the wide-open shot was Marcus's first assist. It felt good to him to know he had made a move, seen the other player come over to him, and then move the ball to his teammate for a basket. It got Marcus to thinking that he might like that idea as much as scoring a basket of his own.

Valerie stepped back to the top, taking the ball with her. This time when she said, "Check ball," and bounced it to Marcus, he knew exactly what to do. He turned around with the ball in his hand, looked at Derek and AJ to see if they were ready, and bounced the ball back to Valerie. Lesson learned.

Valerie passed the ball to Miles this time, to her left, and started his way to set a screen on Derrik.

Marcus was actually the one who yelled "SWITCH, SWITCH," this time as he saw Valerie moving to screen his teammate.

Immediately he picked up Miles on defense as the bigger player was coming around Valerie's screen. Miles wasn't quite as quick as Marcus, and so he took a couple dribbles and passed the ball to his right to Kenny.

Miles then went to set a screen on AJ, who was guarding Kenny.

AJ then yelled "SWITCH, SWITCH," just like he had on the first possession.

Marcus was processing the screens and the switching and trying to mentally keep up with what choices each player had when they came off the screens.

Marcus switched again onto Kenny, feeling a little like a yo-yo.

This time though, Kenny didn't have room to explode to the basket. Marcus was using the "slide drill" Derrik and Kenny had shown him to stay in front of his opponent.

Instead, seeing Marcus playing defense like he should, Kenny passed the ball back to Valerie, who was still on Kenny's left.

After he let go of the ball, Kenny didn't follow his pass by setting a screen on Derrik, who was guarding Valerie.

Instead, Derrik shouted to Marcus, "Switch back."

Marcus realized this meant he would have to step over to guard Valerie where she was, while Derrik stepped over to guard Kenny.

With no screen to use, Valerie slowly dribbled toward Marcus, who was farther away from her than he should have been.

Because Marcus wasn't ready to play tight defense, Valerie stopped her dribble and immediately let go of a long jump shot.

Just like her jumper to start the game, this one was perfect too.

Marcus thought to himself, "I can't back off of her that far. She's too good a shot and if I'm not closer when I'm playing defense, she's gonna score easily."

Marcus had just learned his next lesson. If you aren't willing to get close enough to the action, you probably won't be able to succeed--at whatever you're doing.

For the first time since he started playing ball with these older kids, he thought about how that lesson made sense for his family's situation. He thought about his mom and how she was dealing with Jason, Marcus's older brother.

"Mom's gonna have to stay pretty closely connected with Jason. If she doesn't, she won't have a chance of helping him deal with whatever challenges he's gonna face," he told himself.

Marcus didn't realize it right then, but he had just applied a lesson from basketball to one in his own life. That's where games become really important for kids, when what they learn matters to more than the game.

AJ was at the top this time to put the ball into play. He bounced it to Kenny, who checked to see if Miles and Valerie were ready, and then bounced it back to AJ.

Derrik was on AJ's right, with Marcus on his left. AJ quickly passed to Derrik, and then came toward Marcus. As AJ moved toward him, he motioned for Marcus to come over the screen he was going to set on Valerie.

As soon as Marcus came past AJ's screen, Derrik passed him the ball.

Immediately Kenny switched off of AJ to play defense on Marcus. Marcus wasn't quite sure what to do with the ball until Derrik came to set a screen on Kenny. That meant Miles was switching onto Marcus, who remembered he was quicker than the bigger player.

This time, instead of being able to explode by Miles, Marcus saw out of the corner of his eye, Derrik spinning so Kenny was behind him, while moving straight toward the basket. Marcus instinctively bounced the ball, straight between the taller defender's spread-out legs, for a perfect pass to Derrik, who had an easy right-hand layup to score.

"Yeah dawg!!" Derrik yelled.

"That was a sweet pass Marcus. That's what we call a pick and roll. I set the pick or screen on Kenny, spun a little to get him behind me, and rolled or moved to the basket. I was hopin' you'd see me for the easy pass but goin' between Miles's legs was a little extra style. Nicely done little man!"

Marcus was trying to take in what Derrik described. As he quickly replayed the screen, Miles's switch, Derrik's move to the basket, and his own pass, it made sense how the parts worked together. It was kinda like a puzzle when you find two or three pieces all fitting together. You start to see the finished picture taking shape.

The first game took another 15 minutes or so and Marcus was able to make a couple more nice passes to help his team.

But the sweetest moment was when he caught AJ's pass from the other side of the court, and he saw Valerie coming at him to stop his jump shot.

He gave her a pump fake, pretending like he was going to shoot. She jumped in the air, which gave Marcus room to dribble once to the left side and go up for a jump shot from about 15 feet away. His shot went cleanly through the net.

Right after that, he heard "Ball game!" as Derrik yelled. Marcus hadn't realized that he had just hit the game winner.

AJ and Derrik stepped toward Marcus, lookin' for fist bumps and high fives.

"Sweet move Marcus," AJ offered.

"You were ballin' kid, and we win!!" he declared, more for the other team than for Derrik and Marcus.

All six players went for their water bottles and sat down against the brick wall, under the baskets.

Marcus was all smiles, but he couldn't help but think about the other lessons he'd learned as he played the rest of the game with the older kids. He learned about playing physically when you're on defense, so it's harder for the person you're guarding to get by you.

He also learned about how important it is to communicate while you're actually playing. Derrik was the perfect example of that. He talked all the time, and most of it about what was happening while they played.

As Marcus thought about how much these older players communicated, he started thinking about his family again, and how much they struggled to communicate.

That, of course, led him to think about all the problems his family was having. He thought about how much his mom and dad argued with each other before the separation.

"That wasn't good communication," he thought.

Then he thought about his older brother and how much he was yelling at their mom yesterday.

"That wasn't good communication either."

This was the second time Marcus saw how much what he learned while playing ball was actually making him think about life with his family.

His thoughts shifted back to the game and the other players. They were talkin' smack with each other, laughing a little bit, and drawing his attention away from his family.

He thought again, even more clearly than he did yesterday, how important it was to believe in yourself. If there were more players on the court at one time, there were probably also more defenders who could stop you, or more possible ways to play with your teammates. But that would only happen if your confidence was high enough. If you didn't believe you could do something good with the ball, you wouldn't be valuable to your teammates.

He had also learned how to pass to open shooters through this game.

He had learned how to use his quickness to get by a bigger player, and he had learned that working hard was always gonna lead to something good.

As he sat there smiling and listening to the others, he thought about how so many lessons came from just one game of 3-on-3. Either Marcus was an excellent student, or this game he loved was an excellent teacher.

"Maybe it's both," he thought.

Chapter 17

Advanced Studies, Part 2
(The Same Day at the Courts)

Marcus loved playing with these older kids, even more than he did yesterday.

Today, because there were more players, there were more possibilities. That meant he had even more chances to learn about the game and about himself as a player.

They'd been sitting in the shade for a few minutes when the lessons Marcus would learn headed in a totally different direction.

"Hey Marcus." It was Kenny talking this time.

"It was great havin' you out here with us. Derrik and AJ were right. You do have some sweet skills, for a 7th grader."

He was teasing, and Marcus could see it when Kenny smiled after the last remark.

"No seriously, you beat me off the dribble more than once. You made me pay for helpin' on defense, when you kicked the ball to AJ for the open jumper. That's good ballin' Marcus. And you're tellin' us yesterday was the first time you actually played in a game with other players?"

Marcus had to admit it. He was brand new.

"Yeah, I mean all I've ever done was watch a few games, some on-line videos about ball handling, and then shoot and work on moves in the driveway."

"You ever been to any camps, or worked with any skills coaches?" Valerie asked.

"Most kids, by the time they hit 7th grade, have gone to at least a couple camps, and maybe worked with a skills coach for at least a few sessions."

She was trying to find out a little more about Marcus's basketball background. Like everybody else there, she had a hard time believing Marcus had not played anywhere before he met these guys.

"You did a couple things out there that most players don't learn for quite a while. And they don't learn them without playin' quite a bit of ball. That pick and roll with Derrik, that was instinctive stuff Marcus. Also, when you faked me into the air at the end, that was really good basketball. And then you finished it by knockin' down the shot."

Marcus was feeling comfortable talking with the other players by now.

"Really, you guys are the only coaches I've ever had."

"That might sound kinda funny, but it's true," he continued.

"You guys explain to me so well what needs to happen. The rest of it just makes sense. I see two or three things working together in my mind, and I just play. So when you guys tell me to switch on screens, or to look for mismatches, if I get a chance to think about it for a minute, my mind and body just work together and I can make plays."

"I'm not sure where my connection with how to play basketball came from, except that I love the game. I watched a few NBA games on TV, and I just fell in love with the game. Now, I see the plays people make and I see myself makin' moves like that in my mind."

"But neither one of my parents plays any sports. My older brother and sister don't play any sports either."

Miles was the next of the older kids to reach out.

"So, what's your family like? I mean, are they into how much you love to play ball?"

Marcus was a little slow to respond as he thought about how his family was falling apart. "Well, because yesterday and today are the first times I've actually played with anyone, I guess they don't have a chance to watch me."

"When I used to shoot and dribble a lot in my dad's driveway, my older brother came out and shot with me a couple times, but-"

He hesitated to share too much.

"Well, he always got impatient with me. My older brother is a really smart guy, but he doesn't have patience or time to hang out with a little brother."

"What will they think if they find out my family's a mess?" he asked himself.

From somewhere inside of himself he found the courage to be honest about what he was living through. These older kids just had a way of making him feel safe, like he could share important things with them.

"We don't live with my dad anymore."

Marcus was actually dropping his head as he spoke, avoiding eye contact with any of the older kids.

"So, I'm not sure what my family will think about me playing ball. I hope it matters to them."

The other kids could hear the pain in Marcus's voice and their hearts went out to him.

"Marcus, you don't have to be ashamed." Miles was stepping a bit more meaningfully into the conversation now.

"We all know kids whose parents can't stick together. Most of us here figure if we meet someone dealin' with that kind of pain, we do the best we can to encourage them. If that means we ask them to play ball, ok. But it doesn't have to be just basketball. It could be in school too. We get it. It's hard enough growin' up without your family comin' apart."

Miles didn't realize it but hanging out with others who understood that this divorce wasn't his fault, was exactly what Marcus needed. He needed to hear that people didn't think he was someone to stay away from.

It was so easy to think that no one else was dealing with the same kind of family break-up as his. Instead, here were some kids who barely knew him, helping him to realize he wasn't all alone as his family dealt with its ugliness.

Marcus felt embarrassed as he thought about whether anyone in his family would care about his playing ball.

Just like so many other kids going through their parents' divorce, loneliness was a legitimate challenge. That's another reason Marcus loved hangin' out with these older kids. He wasn't left at his grandparents' house, wondering what to do with himself.

Many kids wrestle with loneliness because of the sense of loss they feel. Just like Marcus, a child's sense of self-worth is directly connected to how secure their family situation is. If that family dynamic starts to crumble, kids feel incomplete, and ashamed of what they're becoming.

Adults are right to focus on the loneliness a child experiences as they go through their parents' divorce. That growing sense of isolation becomes a huge contributor toward lower levels of confidence for children, which can lead to all kinds of other challenges.

While Marcus was playing ball, his confidence was high, especially as he was learning more and more about the game. It was in situations like he was experiencing now, where he had to think or talk about his family's reality, when he struggled to feel good about himself. Hearing the kindness in the older kids' voices, and their willingness to encourage him, made it easier to trust.

"You guys just don't know how much it means for you to let me talk. You may not know it, but what you're saying right now is what I needed to hear. My family had a really hard day yesterday. What I saw, with my mom feeling so much pain, well, coming out here to play ball with you guys, and now being able to hear you talk like this, it makes me feel so much better. It's like the problems go away when you can share them with someone else."

Miles continued. "It's all good Marcus. Our parents have taught us to work hard at whatever we do, to treat others respectfully, and to care about each other. Pretty simple really. Actually, it's what we've seen from the life of Christ for most of our lives."

"Our parents have told us that the lessons we learn from his example need to be what others see in us. They've told us that our lives have to be real, not just talk. So you see, you're actually doin' us a favor. You're givin' us the chance to practice what we've been taught. ``

AJ began speaking. "I don't know about everyone else, but it feels good to know we can help you deal with your family pain. Oh, and you can ball with us anytime."

AJ had a softness to him, even though he was really competitive. Of all the players here, Marcus felt the most comfortable with him.

The beautiful interaction between Marcus and the older kids ended as quickly as it had begun, as Marcus saw--and heard--a group of four older boys approaching the court where the players were sitting.

"Derrik, what are you doin' here?" The obvious leader of the group called out from across the court.

His question didn't sound friendly. Instead, it was more of an accusation, and right away everyone was on edge.

"We ain't doin' nothin' man, just playin' some ball."

Derrik was quick to respond, but he didn't immediately get up. It felt like he didn't really want to connect with this older boy.

The older boy continued. "Let's see, you got Miles and Kenny here, two of my brothers. You got, is that AJ? I ain't seen you in forever AJ. What are you doin' man?"

"I'm hangin' with these players," AJ responded quickly, but just like Derrik, he didn't sound comfortable about the exchange.

The older boy scanned the group and started again, only this time with an edge to his voice.

"Then you got a girl playin' ball with you guys? Have I ever met her before? What's your name girl?"

"I'm Valerie. I moved here a year or so ago and I've been playin' ball with these guys ever since. We met at school, and I found out they play tournament ball. That's what I wanted to do so they asked me to join."

Valerie was a confident girl, and not just from playing ball with the guys. But the older boy had even made her uncomfortable.

Next the older boy looked at Marcus.

"And what you doin' hangin' with a White kid, D?"

He looked over his shoulder at Derrik as he asked. This whole exchange was already uncomfortable for Marcus, but when he heard the words ``a White kid,'' that's when the knot in Marcus's stomach really started to tighten.

Marcus was watching the other players as the questions came. Their faces were looking just as uncomfortable as his stomach felt. In fact, they were shaking their heads back and forth slowly, exchanging glances. Maybe they were wondering what was going to happen, just like Marcus was. Was this gonna get ugly?

"Oh, I hope not. We were havin' such a good time," Marcus told himself.

Maybe Derrik understood the need to do something quickly, because he stood up and started across the court, toward the older boys.

Asserting himself, Derrik said, "This is Marcus. AJ and I met him yesterday. Played a little ball with him. He's younger than us, but the kid has sweet skills. That's why we asked him to come back today. AJ and I brought the rest with us so we could play more than 21."

It was a little like Derrik was trying to prove something to the older boy, but what, Marcus wasn't sure.

Derrik walked closer to the group, away from the players, but Marcus could still hear what he said.

"Man, why you have to come around here messin' with the good time we're havin'? We're trying to make it comfortable for Marcus and you have to bring up race. He's the only White kid here and now he's gonna feel totally singled out. Why's it always have to be about race with you DeShaun? And why you have to call out someone like that?"

Marcus admired Derrik's confidence. This was a tense situation, and Derrik was sticking up for him. He stepped right into the middle of it instead of trying to avoid it.

His questions to the older boy seemed to hit a sensitive spot. The older boy fired back at Derrik, and this is where it started to feel really intense.

"D, you know everything's about race anymore. That's the world we live in. When you start mixin' with people who know nothin' about how you live, or what you have to deal with every day, you know you're gonna run into somethin' ugly. You're gonna hear people talkin' about you. You'll hear rumors around the neighborhood if you're not careful."

"You watch, D. You keep hangin' with this kid and White folk will start askin' questions about what's up with you and their little man. They can't see us the way we see each other. That's the way it is. It's always an issue."

There was some part of what the older boy was saying that really stuck with Marcus. He had never actually had any non-White friends. And here he was, sitting with five older kids, and each one of them was from a different race than his own.

It's not that he didn't want to have non-White friends. It's just that at his grade school, almost everyone came from the same neighborhood, and almost everyone was White. In his entire grade school, he could remember maybe three kids who weren't White.

Mostly, Marcus just never gave the whole idea of races mixing with each other any thought. He played with his White friends because they all came from the same neighborhood, and because they all had the same interests.

As he thought about it more, Marcus realized the biggest reason he was so comfortable hangin' with these older kids is because they kinda came from a similar background too.

They all came from basketball. They all loved basketball.

"Wasn't that enough?" he asked himself.

"Wasn't that enough to make it so that your skin color doesn't matter?"

In Marcus's 12-year-old mind, basketball was big enough to make any differences go away.

Derrik turned away from the older kids and started walking back to the others. His face didn't look very happy. Shortly after that, the older boys started walking away also.

"Hey everybody, I'm sorry about DeShaun," Derrik said after the older kids were gone.

"Everyone in this school knows him and everyone knows what he's about. He's always doin' the same thing. He starts talking about ugliness between the races, instead of trying to do something positive about it."

"We know," Miles and Kenny volunteered.

"Thanks for steppin' up D, for everybody else. We just didn't want it to get ugly with him and his boys."

"I hear you," Derrik replied.

"Ya know, I've only seen DeShaun and his boys get physical with someone else one time, and it seems like they yelled at each other quite a bit before anything actually happened."

"Guess I didn't want that to happen here, not now. We're havin' a good time with each other, and I didn't want it to be ruined by somebody comin' around and makin' an issue out of race."

Derrik continued. "Valerie, I'm so sorry you got disrespected. You are totally cool with everyone here. Don't you ever doubt that. And you make the rest of us better on the court. I mean it V."

"Not a problem D. I been competin' with guys a long time and I hear them sayin' a lot of things I wish they wouldn't."

"You guys probably don't know it, but when we play in tournaments, some of the things I have to listen to are just ugly. So many guys think that because I'm a girl, I have no right to play in tournaments with you guys."

"But I choose to play with you guys instead of in girls' tournaments. It just makes me a stronger player. And I know when we play high school ball, and I have to match up against older girls, hangin' with you guys is gonna make me able to compete right away."

"But because guys on other teams say inappropriate things sometimes, mostly I've learned to keep my ears shut, and my mind focused on basketball."

"I also know you don't see a lot of Asian players in tournaments, guys or girls. So, in one way I'm used to it, being a girl and Asian. In another way, I wish we would get to the point where people can see each of us for who we are. People just hopin' to play ball and havin' a good time hangin' with friends."

She continued. "As long as people make an issue out of things like race or whether girls are good enough to play with the guys, we're gonna see people like DeShaun makin' too many of us uncomfortable."

Marcus couldn't have guessed what he would get to be a part of as he was heading to the school today. He knew he'd learn something about basketball, playing with older kids. But what he was hearing now was way beyond that.

He didn't watch much news, but he had heard about enough of the protesting going on around the country for the last year or two to know that different races were having serious problems with each other.

Now, sitting and listening to these older kids talk--and watching Derrik's and DeShaun's exchange--made him start thinking about racial interaction differently. Growing up where he did, it just never was an issue.

Maybe what was most impressive to Marcus in all of this, was how much confidence each of these older players talked with. Listening to Valerie talk about being a girl and an Asian made him realize how little he knew about the world around him.

AJ spoke up. "Marcus, DeShaun is two years older than we are. He's supposed to be going into 11th grade at the high school, but I don't know if he's already dropped out, or whether he's still there."

"When we were 6th graders, he was the loudest voice at school here, and not really the best one for us to listen to. At assemblies, in the hallways, in the cafeteria, seems like he was always bringing up the idea that racial disrespect happens everywhere. Each one of us here has heard from him more times than we can remember."

Kenny spoke next. He had the kindest voice of all of them.

"One thing all of us need to keep in mind is that DeShaun probably hasn't had the same experiences we have. He's probably got some ugliness that our parents have kept us away from."

"Because of that, it's probably important to at least hear what DeShaun says. But our parents have also taught us to be part of a solution. That's where we might be different from DeShaun and his boys. Maybe all they know is anger or hatred. Maybe yellin' is what they hear most of all at home. Maybe they hear their moms or dads talking about ugliness between the races, and that's all he knows to say."

Kenny continued. "Marcus, whether you're White or non-White, what matters to us is what kind of person you are--and whether you can ball. Just jokin', but that does make it easier."

"Every one of us wants to be the best ball player and the best person we can. That's all that really matters. I'm sorry DeShaun called you out. It had nothin' to do with you, and everything to do with the way he sees the world."

Chapter 18

Look at It from My Side

Marcus had no idea he was going to learn so much at the playground in one short afternoon. This was a lot for him to process. He felt like he had the basketball lessons down really well. But what he was hearing about race from these guys--and how Valerie had to deal with a lot of ugly remarks about playing in guys' tournaments, instead of girls', all of this was more than he had hoped for.

As he sat and listened, and he thought about how kind these older kids were, he knew he needed to ask them some questions.

Maybe it was his natural curiosity. His mom and grandma had said many times that he wanted to know as much as he could about so many different things. Maybe that's what he was feeling now.

He spoke up respectfully. "Do you guys think there's any truth to what DeShaun was sayin'? Do you think some white people wonder if it's a good thing for different races to mix too much with each other, especially when it's kids?"

Miles was the first to respond.

"My mom and dad grew up in Southern California, in the middle of the city. It was definitely a Black neighborhood."

"They tell me when they were kids, they just didn't see many Whites in their part of the city. They grew up with this idea that Whites and Blacks just didn't mix. It wasn't really about whether they should or not. They just didn't. It's just not what their neighborhood was about."

He continued, but more with his own voice now. More with what he felt, not just what he was told.

"The one thing my parents have told me to do, again and again, is to be respectful to all people, no matter what they look like, or where they come from."

Miles had much more to say.

"My parents have also told me and my brothers that they've had some ugly things said to them. They've been called ugly names, and yeah, most of it has come from White people. And it hurts, like it would anybody else, ya know."

"But they have also told us that we cannot think that all White people are like that. I mean, check this out, you're sittin' here with us, and it's totally comfortable. What my parents really want us to understand is that people of every color have challenges, and people of every color are worth connecting with."

"DeShaun will have a hard time thinking any White people will be ok with him because all he can see is color differences. We can't do that, no matter what the color of our skin is. We have to be able to see people as people, not as this color or that color."

"Ya know Marcus," Miles continued, "One of the most important lessons my parents emphasize from the life of Christ is the idea of loving your neighbor. They don't say our neighbors are just the people who look like us or live like us. They say our neighbors are everyone and anyone we connect with. Because of that position, we just don't think about racial differences causing division between people."

AJ wanted to share as well. "My parents came from Mexico when they were young. By the time they were in grade school, they were the only Hispanics in their classes. But by the time they reached high school, there were a lot of others with similar backgrounds."

"Their history doesn't mean they haven't had ugly things said to them, just like Miles's parents, but they have told me and my sister that it was easier to mix with Whites when they were kids."

"When they were in school, especially if they went to school with White kids for many years in a row, they were just the same as any of the other kids. The White kids didn't see them as different. At least that's what they felt it was like. Everybody was in the same class, doing the same work and playing the same games. It wasn't until they got out of school and started working that they started seeing people making a big deal about racial differences."

"Now we have so much talk about immigration in the US, and a wall at the Mexican border. Because my family is from there and look at me, a lot of people got it figured out that my family is not from here. But because we're from Mexico, and because a lot of people only see Hispanics as Mexicans, instead of from a lot of different countries or cultures, my parents have heard some really ugly things. Actually, so have I."

"But I'm with Miles. My parents will not let me and my sister say anything negative about races mixing together. They tell us again and again to only focus on the good things that happen between people. The message has really stuck with us. We will be positive even if that's not what's happening around us."

Valerie wanted to share from her experience.

"I love what you guys are sayin', about kids being able to see each other as just kids, and about respecting all people. But it's not as easy as it sounds."

Marcus appreciated Valerie; he really wanted to hear what she had to say.

"My mom has told me about how hard it was for her growing up in Vietnam. You see, in my parents' country, even the slightest difference can make you stand out. If you're from the north and you visit the south, people see you as different and sometimes treat you as less than they are. It's the same thing if it's the other way around."

"But add to that the fact that she's a woman. She has shared that many times she would hear men say mean or really inappropriate things to her--in Vietnam and here in the US. It started when she was even younger than we are."

"I guess what I'm sayin' is that there are people in this world who will pick you out for being different, and make you feel uncomfortable. It might be because of race, but it could also be because of your gender."

"But just like Miles and AJ have said, my mom has made sure that my sister and I understand we have a choice. We get to choose whether we let others make us feel small, or whether we will be confident, no matter what anyone else says. I hear her voice in my head every day. It sticks. What DeShaun was trying to do, it doesn't matter."

Marcus could tell Derrik was thinking hard about what the others were saying. He listened to each of his friends speak, sometimes nodding his head, other times biting his lower lip, like he did when he missed the jump shot yesterday and shaking his head from side to side.

After Valerie finished talking, Derrick started in.

"I have an uncle who's in prison. He was arrested about five years ago for stealing something from another person's apartment. My dad isn't sure that his brother is actually guilty of what he was charged with."

"When the trial was taking place, and I was 8 or 9 when it happened, I remember my mom and dad talking after my brother and I went to bed. They talked about how people in the courtroom were saying things like, 'It was a Black man I saw running out of the yard,' and 'Yeah, but it could have been any Black man.' For some reason, those things have really stuck with me."

"I know I don't want to be negative about race," Derrik continued, "but there are times when I know being Black will make some other people think certain things about you without actually getting to know you. That's when it gets hard to be that person who sees beyond race."

"Look, my parents have done a pretty good job of raising my brother and me to be good with anyone, whatever their race is. But I'll be honest with you guys. There are times where I struggle with it. I hear somebody like DeShaun sayin' people will start talkin' or spreading rumors. That's when it isn't easy. But I know I want to be part of the solution, not the problem."

Marcus had lived his entire life in an isolated community, one where challenges that 12-year-olds in other places had to face just didn't happen. This would take some time to process.

As he sat there with the others, listening to them talk about DeShaun and what he'd said, Marcus started feeling thankful. Here he was, a 12-year-old without a home, with a chance to meet other kids with different lives than his. And they were accepting him for just who he was, no matter how messed up his family was. No matter what color his skin was.

Some experiences are more important than others in people's lives. Marcus, only 12 years old, had a pretty good idea this was one of those. Talking with the older players, being able to share his pain about his family, and hearing the way their parents helped them to understand racial issues, these were ideas and conversations that would change how he saw the world. He may not know exactly what those changes would look like, but he knew they would happen.

Chapter 19

Basketball and Life

After spending so much time talking about families and racial issues, the kids just wanted to play some more ball.

For the next game of 3 on 3, they mixed up the teams a little. Marcus would play with Miles and Valerie, while AJ, Derrik, and Kenny would play together.

Marcus's basketball lessons kept going. That's part of what it means to play with others. You learn about what they can do, where they feel most confident on the floor, and how their skills work with your own. This was Marcus's learning for the second game.

After the game finished, the older players were ready to get home. That left Marcus and his basketball, with the court to himself. This "aloneness" made it easier to think about all that had happened.

He took his ball, started working on some dribble combinations, and got busy processing what had happened.

Thoughts entered and left his mind quickly, sometimes bringing understanding. Other times creating more questions.

One idea that kept coming back to him was how much talking about racial mixing made him think about differences in his own family. He thought about his older brother and how he could never take much interest in what Marcus cared about. They were both smart kids, but in very different areas.

"I wonder if I could've done something to be more interested in what he cared about?" Marcus asked himself.

His brother was gone from their family now and Marcus didn't know if he'd see him again. The idea bothered him, but not because his older brother was nice to him. It was because his family was now that much more broken apart.

Marcus also thought about how different his parents were. His dad didn't seem to do anything but work, and his mom tried every way she could to make life better for Marcus and his siblings.

"Maybe those differences were too much for them to stay together," he thought out loud.

This was the first time Marcus felt like he was making a little sense of his family's situation.

"Looks like basketball is my teacher again. But this time it's not about the game. It's about my life."

Marcus was a smart kid, but what mattered was his finding how to apply what he learned from what he loved--basketball--to what his life was like every day. What his mom or grandma couldn't explain to him about why things happened, he was actually learning more clearly from the game he couldn't get enough of.

The afternoon was getting a little late, so Marcus took his water bottle and ball, and started the three-block dribble to his grandparents' house.

When something really matters, you can't stop thinking about it. When you go to bed, it's still in your mind. When you get up and get busy with something else, it keeps coming in and out of your mind. That happened as he started walking.

He had left the school parking lot and walked about half a block when he saw DeShaun and the older kids walking toward him.

"Oh no, is this gonna be okay?" he quickly asked himself.

His walking slowed down, but he didn't want to stop or go to the other side of the street. Instead, he lowered his head and kept walking.

"Hey kid, Marcus, isn't it?" DeShaun was callin' him out as they approached each other. "Hey, let me ask you a question. How come you, a White kid, wanna hang with my boys, D, Kenny, and Miles?"

DeShaun kept pushing. "I mean, aren't you more comfortable playin' ball with other White kids? Don't you wonder if one of my brothers is gonna start messin' with ya? I mean that's what most White folks think of Blacks, isn't it?"

"Ya know kid, I expected you to walk to the other side of the street when you saw me and my boys comin' toward you. That's what most White folks do."

Marcus was not ready for this. Just like Derrik had said after the first interaction with DeShaun, this guy really wanted to make it about racial issues.

His thoughts were a little shaky.

"I was havin' such a good time, learning so much about so many things, and now DeShaun is making me really uncomfortable," he thought as he fished for a response.

"I'm only 12 DeShaun and really, I don't think about races mixing with each other the same way you do. I love basketball and I guess the other guys do too. That's all it is. It doesn't feel like it has to be anything else."

"Yeah, that's all good, you guys can ball together. But what if those kids wanted to do other things with you, like goin' to a movie, or hangin' together at one of their houses? Would you be cool with that?"

Marcus hadn't thought about anything more than basketball; but hangin' out with the other players in other places sounded pretty good to him.

"I think I would love to hang out with the other players away from basketball. They are so nice to me. And my life is kinda messed up right now. They really helped me to think about it in different ways."

"Ya know kid," DeShaun continued, "I have had a lot of ugly things said to me as I walk around this neighborhood. I've seen people close their curtains when I walk by their house, or I can hear doors bein' locked. Most of those things come from White folks."

"I've wondered what it is about bein' Black that makes people uncomfortable. So you can see why I spend time talkin' about race so much. I live in the middle of it every day. You may not like what I'm sayin', but this is reality for a lot of us."

"When I was about your age, maybe a little younger, my dad sat me down and told me what I needed to do to keep people from messin' with me. He was definitely talkin' about the cops, but he was also talkin' about a lot of other people."

"Your dad ever sit you down for that kinda talk? Anyone ever told you that if you go into a store, you can't put your hands in your pockets? They ever told you to keep your hands where the store owner can always see 'em?"

"You see, this is what we deal with every day. Me and my brothers. So many people figure that as Blacks, we're more dangerous. More likely to steal somethin' than White people. Do you have any idea how that makes us feel? It ain't good."

"I'm sorry." It was all Marcus could think to say.

He had never thought about the kind of things DeShaun was saying. He had never thought about how being White meant there were some things he would never have to deal with.

"I am so sorry you have to deal with those things DeShaun. But I don't do those things and I never would. All I want is to get to know people and have a good time with them. It doesn't matter to me what color their skin is."

DeShaun seemed to be softening a little with Marcus.

"I appreciate that little man. Really, I do. I want you to do something for me. I want you to tell every White person you know how great it is to hang with D, Kenny, and Miles. I want you to tell people how much they care about you, how smart they are, and how hard they work."

"Ya' see, I figure if more and more White folks hear good things about young Blacks, maybe it'll make just a little difference in how they see all of us. Can you do that for me?"

Marcus was feeling a lot better about where this was going.

"I will DeShaun. These older guys I played with today were so good to me, it's gonna be easy to tell people good things about them."

"Hey DeShaun, thanks for talkin' to me. It means a lot."

"You got it little man," DeShaun responded, as he and his friends started walking away.

"Be cool and keep workin' on that game."

Chapter 20

Takin' It Home

"Wow. That's not what I expected," Marcus told himself.

He now had even more to think about as he walked back to his grandparents'. He had all those lessons from basketball that made sense for his family. But now he had lessons about Whites and Blacks. What DeShaun said really stuck with him.

"DeShaun is right. Nobody has ever told me things I can't do in stores or to worry about police officers. In fact, nobody has ever told me there was anything I needed to be careful about when I was out in public doin' things."

"He was also right about people moving to the other side of the street. I actually thought about doing that when I saw him, but it wasn't because he was Black. It was because what he said earlier made me uncomfortable."

There was still an awful lot that didn't make sense to Marcus, but he could live with that. He didn't have to have all the answers right now.

As Marcus turned into his grandparents' driveway, he started to feel how tired he was. It was a long day at the middle school, and how much he'd been through started to weigh on him.

He opened the back door to the kitchen, where his grandma spent so much time.

"Hi Grandma. I'm tired."

"Oh Marcus, it's good to see you. We were beginning to wonder if we needed to make a trip down to the school, to see if you were there. It's been over three hours since you left"

"I'm sorry Grandma. I'm sure I lost track of time. Besides, I feel like today was one of the most important days of my life."

"It sounds like the kind of thing you probably need to share with someone Marcus."

His grandma was always curious; today she seemed a little more like concerned.

"Please sit down and tell me about what happened."

"Sure," Marcus said. "But can I get a drink of water first?"

"Of course. I'll be at the table, waiting for you."

Marcus joined her and immediately asked a question.

"Grandma, do you think White people have an easier life than Black people?"

She didn't respond immediately, but she could see how serious her grandson was about the question.

"That's an awfully important question Marcus. Did something happen at the school today that led you to ask it?"

"Yeah," he quickly responded.

"I played basketball with some older Black kids today. I met one of them yesterday and he was so nice to me. I was pretty excited when I saw him again today. He actually had some other players with him too. There was a kid from Mexico and a girl from Vietnam there too. But there were three Black players."

"We finished one game and were talking about some different things, when a group of older Black kids walked by. One of them started asking questions and making all of us kinda uncomfortable."

"He started talkin' about how Blacks and Whites don't mix with each other very much. He even said they probably shouldn't mix much."

"Well, that didn't last too long as one of the guys I was playing with went over to the older kids and started talking to them. After a few minutes Derrik, he's the one I played ball with yesterday, came back to where we were. After that the older kids left."

"Well, that whole conversation with the older kids made the rest of us talk an awful lot about race, and how life is different for people who aren't White."

"The kids I played ball with all shared what their parents have told them about being from a different race, but they also shared what their own feelings are."

"I have never had the chance to talk with people from another race like I did today. It was amazing Grandma."

"As I started walking back here after we finished playing another game, I saw the older kids who made us feel uncomfortable coming toward me."

"You didn't have any problems with these older boys, did you Marcus?"

Her voice was shaking just a little.

"No, but I was definitely a little nervous when I saw them, and they saw me."

"Anyway, I kept walking toward them. Something inside me told me not to walk to the other side of the street. It just felt like I needed to stay where I was and deal with whatever happened."

"As I came to them, the guy who did most of the talking, his name is DeShaun, asked me some questions about why I would want to hang out with Black kids instead of White."

"At first, I didn't know what to say. But then DeShaun started telling me about things he has had to deal with as a young Black guy. He said his dad has had to talk to him about what you can and can't do to keep White people from thinking you might do something wrong."

"But then, he asked me something that really made me think. He asked if anyone has ever had to talk to me about how to act when I'm around the police or in stores, and I realized no one ever has."

"I have never had people walk to the other side of the street when they see me coming toward them. I have never had to worry about keeping my hands where people can see them when I go into a store. I have never had people call me ugly names. I have never heard people locking their doors when they see me walking by their house."

"So this is why I'm asking you this question now. This is why I'm wondering if as a White kid, I have it easier, you know, with what people say and how they treat me, than the Black kids I met today."

"That was quite a day for you Marcus. And all that in only about three hours. Isn't it amazing how something that happens so quickly can be so important?"

His grandma was now thinking out loud, her mind on Marcus's question and his older sister at the same time.

"I don't know very much about what you've asked Marcus," she admitted.

"I have had only a couple non-White friends in my life, and no African-American friends. It wasn't that I didn't want them as friends. I just didn't have opportunities. We didn't know any Black families."

"We have lived in this neighborhood and haven't really met many people during the last 30 or 40 years except our neighbors right next to us, or maybe two or three houses away."

"Grandma," Marcus was ready to share more.

"I started thinking the same thing as I was listening to the older kids at the playground today."

"At my dad's house, when I was little, everybody in the neighborhood, and almost everybody at the elementary school was White. I just didn't have chances to know kids who weren't. It wasn't that I didn't want to. I just didn't think about it--until today."

"DeShaun asked me to do something just before we were finished talking. He asked me to tell every White person I can how smart, and how hard-working, and how caring the three Black kids I played ball with are."

"He said maybe if I tell a lot of people, then maybe a few more White people will start to see young Black guys more positively. Do you think that could really be true?"

"Oh Marcus, I am so proud of you." His grandma's eyes were watering a little.

"You have had a chance that so many of us don't get. You have had a chance to see the world from someone's else's position. Someone whose life is very different from your own."

"You also have a chance to be an example of how we are challenged to see the world. So many belief systems tell us that humans--all humans--have the same value. We know that in our hearts. But it isn't until we start interacting with people who are different than ourselves, that we actually get to put those beliefs into practice."

"We focus so much on our differences; it makes us forget about the things we have in common. We seem to forget the fact that each of us, no matter our color, our language, our families, or even what religious beliefs we have, or even if we have any, each of us lives and breathes with the same body parts. Remember this Marcus: we are all people with infinite value."

She continued. "I said I didn't know much about what you asked, and that's true. But I do know what DeShaun asked you to do is terribly important. I have a feeling there are a lot of White people who don't think an awful lot about how challenging it is to be a non-White person. You have a chance to change that Marcus. I hope you will."

Chapter 21

Another Bomb Drops

When Marcus walked up to his grandparents' back door, he didn't notice the bright red car parked along the street in front of the house. His mind was still focused on what had happened at the middle school that afternoon.

But as he stepped into the house, and finished talking with his grandma, he began to see there was something more going on with his family.

Marcus heard talking coming from the living room. As his mind shifted to what was being said, he heard his mom's voice, his older sister's, and a voice he didn't recognize.

"What's going on in there?" he asked himself.

Part of him thought it might be better to stay in the dining room. Another part wanted to find out what was happening.

As he got up and stepped into the living room doorway, Marcus could see his sister and an older boy holding hands on the couch, while his mom sat in a chair across from them, her eyes red from crying.

"Oh no, not again" he thought.

All he could see was his mom's pain.

"Mom, are you okay?" Marcus asked.

"Honey, I'm talking with your sister and her friend. Marcus, this is Aaron. He and your sister came over to talk this afternoon."

"Hi. It's nice to meet you."

"But Mom, it looks like you've been crying. Are you okay?"

Marcus watched his mother's eyes shift from his to his sister's, and back again.

"Marcus," for some reason his mom hesitated. "I can't really share right now what's going on."

She was talking slowly now.

"Your sister and I have been trying to figure some things out. She and Aaron needed some help with a challenge they have, and they came to me."

"Okay," Marcus continued. "But why have you been crying?"

It wasn't really like Marcus to be pushy, but he had seen his mom in pain often enough since his parents separated, to make him uncomfortable staying quiet.

"Marcus," his mom continued. "You know we've had some challenges since we left your dad's house. This is one more--and we will get through this one too."

It was in this moment that Marcus saw a glimpse of who his mom really was. She was faced with another life-changing moment in her children's lives, she was overcome with pain, yet she spoke with grace and patience, as she sought to help Marcus be at peace.

Because of his mom's dignity and strength, and her willingness to love her children unconditionally, Marcus was feeling he needed to stop pushing for more info. Maybe he'd find out later what was going on. For now, he needed to give his mom a hug.

Walking over to her, Marcus saw for the first time that his sister had been crying too.

Stopping to look at Kristin's face, Marcus felt the need to ask if she was okay. This was the same sister who took such good care of him when his knee ripped open. This was the same sister he used to take riding on his dirt-bike, finding one adventure after another.

"Kristin, are you okay?" Marcus asked.

"Not really," she replied. "Aaron and I aren't sure what to do. We needed to talk to mom."

"What is it?" Marcus pressed.

"I don't want you guys to have problems."

"Thanks for caring, Marcus," Kristin shared. "But we needed to talk to mom. Aaron and I have been seeing each other for a couple months, and, well, I'm pregnant."

That statement caught Marcus off guard and he stood staring at his older sister.

"Did she just say what I thought she said?" he asked himself.

He looked at his mom, almost as an instinct, and could see her eyes start to water again.

"Did you just say you were pregnant Kristin?" He was now talking out loud.

"Did you just say you were pregnant?" He didn't realize he was repeating himself.

"Yeah, I did say that Marcus. Aaron's 17, and I'm only 14. We don't really know what to do and so we needed to talk to Mom."

Marcus continued. "Well, what are you gonna do? I mean, are you gonna have a baby?" It wasn't excitement in his voice; it was confusion.

At 12 he didn't understand much about what it meant to be pregnant, except that a girl was carrying a baby. He definitely didn't understand what was involved in having a baby. What 7th grader did?

"We don't really know what we're gonna do, Marcus," Kristin responded. "That's why we're here. This is too big for us to figure out on our own."

Marcus definitely didn't understand what it meant for a girl to be pregnant. He didn't understand even more what it meant for a 14-year-old.

He didn't understand that when someone that young gets pregnant, they are a child carrying a child.

Marcus didn't understand that his sister, the one he played games with so many times, was now forced to begin her life as an adult, long before she actually became one.

All of these things were a mystery to Marcus, but the one thing he did understand was that his sister needed him and the rest of their family if she was going to make it through this challenge.

Chapter 22

If We Stick Together. . .

After the shock of his sister being pregnant passed, Marcus found himself wanting to help.

"What can I do? I want to help in some way, any way."

He was asking his mom and his sister.

"Marcus," his mom answered. "The best thing you can do right now is to be an excellent brother. It's probably a lot like being an excellent teammate, and I know you know how to do that. That means first of all listening to your sister so you can figure out what she needs."

His mom continued, "We also need to help Kristin and Aaron figure out some details before we know anything specific we can do."

"Marcus," Kristin needed to share something.

"I love you little brother, but I don't want the challenges we have getting in the way of anything you might do."

"Jason's already gone. I don't want this family falling apart anymore because of me. We need to stick together."

For the rest of the day and into the night, Marcus couldn't stop thinking about what his sister had shared.

"How are they gonna do this?" he asked himself, over and over.

And each time, the same "I don't know" filled his mind.

Kristin was 14 and was supposed to start her 9th grade year in the fall.

"Was that plan all messed up now?" he asked himself.

"Was Kristin gonna have to drop out of school?"

Marcus knew enough about school and how important it was. He was also pretty sure Jason wouldn't finish high school, now that he had left the family. Would Kristin follow their older brother's example?

Staying in school was only one of his sister's challenges. Would she and Aaron have their own home, or would they live with the family? Was Aaron still in school?

And would he be able to stay in school now, or would he have to get a job to support Kristin and the baby?

Later that night, with so many questions playing through his mind, Marcus lay in his bed--on the living room floor--for hours. Sleep wouldn't come.

His mind played the same living room scene from earlier in the day, again and again. His mom's swollen, watery eyes, his sister and her boyfriend, sitting on the couch holding hands. The images and the questions that followed wouldn't stop repeating.

It was sometime in the middle of the night when he realized something so clearly, he sat up straight, in the darkness and the quiet.

His mom mentioned it earlier, when Marcus was asking questions. His sister even mentioned it when she said she didn't want the family coming apart any more than it had already.

In that middle-of-the-night moment, when not even the summer crickets were singing, Marcus realized what it meant to stick together. It was as real as the darkness around him, as easy to touch and understand as the skin on his hand.

Marcus Lambert, 12 years old and the product of a separated family with more than its share of pain, realized that no matter what you faced, no matter how intimidating it was, how uncomfortable it was, how scary it was, you stayed with your family.

In that moment with his thoughts the only voice he could hear, Marcus realized that a commitment to your team was all that mattered. He realized that if even one member of the family stepped out of the circle, it would break. It might be a crack at first, but sooner or later it would break.

And it was in that moment that Marcus Lambert made his first "all in" commitment of the heart. He was going to be the best brother possible. To Kristin sure, but also to Maddie and to Jason, if he ever got the chance. He would listen when they talked. He would be the first one to offer help if one of them needed it. He would communicate as much as possible, so they knew what he was thinking, and so he could learn what they needed.

Marcus had made this "all in" commitment to his family, to be the best brother and son possible. What he didn't understand fully was that he was also making an "all in" commitment to doing what was right--in all things. In the stillness of the night, with no distractions and no conflicting emotions, Marcus was opening his heart. He was preparing to serve.

Marcus lay back down, looking into the nothingness above him. With clarity in his mind, he could now see that before tonight, he hadn't thought of his family as his team. Every member, his sisters, his mom, his grandparents, his brother, he was here to support every one of them, and that's what he was gonna do.

Sleep finally came for Marcus, but as his mind drifted, he instinctively started blending the lessons he'd learned while playing basketball with how his sister needed to trust in the people around her. In his 12-year old's mind, she needed to see him and his family as her teammates.

Chapter 23

Advanced Applications

"We can't do that. We have to see if there's another option."

The voices were fuzzy at first, but as they continued, Marcus started to make sense of their words.

It was his mom and grandma, in the kitchen, talking about what happened yesterday. Marcus didn't know it, but someone had already suggested that Kristin consider an abortion, instead of carrying the baby the full nine months of pregnancy.

Abortion becomes an option for many teen mothers if they live in a state that offers them, and if they don't have a support system in place, helping them to work through all of the challenges of having a baby.

Marcus's mom and grandma weren't excited about Kristin having a baby at 14 or 15-years old, but they didn't want to consider the idea of an abortion either. A young woman who hadn't even begun high school was not ready to wrestle with something as serious as this.

They realized an abortion would almost certainly leave Kristin with deep grief over what she'd lost. That choice would also lead her to doubt whether this developing baby was actually a gift.

At only 14 or 15, she wasn't emotionally ready for those questions. As her mother and grandmother, they weren't comfortable with the idea of her having to deal with that much emotional pressure.

For a few moments, Marcus lay in bed, letting his head clear. He thought back to how hard it was to fall asleep, and how making a commitment to his family was so clear in the midnight darkness.

"It wasn't a dream, I'm pretty sure," he told himself.

"What I remember makes so much sense. Kristin needs to know that every one of us is ready to help her and Aaron."

Marcus slowly crawled out of bed and headed to the bathroom to wash up.

"Mom, Grandma, I couldn't sleep for the longest time last night," he shared, as he entered the dining room.

"I was laying in bed, wide awake. I couldn't stop thinking about Kristin and Aaron, and about Jason leaving. I was just laying there until I realized something. I started seeing our family like a basketball team, where everybody has to do whatever they can to make sure the team can win. Once I saw things that way, I was able to fall asleep."

"Marcus," his mom began, "I love your thinking, son. Every one of us is going to have to support those two. They're too young to have a baby and raise a family on their own. I'm also glad you were able to make sense of this challenge in a way that works for you."

She continued. "Let's get you some breakfast so you can get started with your day."

After he'd eaten, Marcus started thinking about basketball again. It was this beautiful combination of what he loved, and how he made sense of his life.

"Mom, Grandma, I want to go down to the playground again today. Do you think that's okay? I mean, do you think I can do that and not miss out on any chance to help with the family?"

He had spent more than three hours at the playground yesterday. Today, he might not have that much time.

"Marcus, until we know exactly what we can or need to do, you can still go to the playground. Those older kids you've told us about sound like such a good influence on you, we don't want you to miss out on being with them."

As always, his grandma's concern was his well-being.

"Thanks Grandma. I'll try not to spend the whole day there. But I do love to play, and because it's only three blocks away, it's super easy to get there."

After helping clean up the kitchen, Marcus grabbed his basketball and went outside to work on his ball handling.

He watched a video a couple days earlier that talked about working on his non-dominant hand without the other hand getting in the way.

Focusing only on the left hand, Marcus took his right hand and put it in his front pocket. He left it there while he started dribbling with the left hand.

He imagined he was facing a defender who was forcing him to go left with the dribble. Concentrating on the fake defender in front of him, Marcus took two hard dribbles and exploded with extra speed to the left side. He repeated this drill again and again, until he could do it without any hesitation.

After a few minutes, Marcus decided to add an element to the drill. Now, instead of just exploding past the fake defender, he would build in a secondary move, in case the defender cut off his first move.

Beginning with his left hand, Marcus exploded past the defender again. Only this time, he crossed his dribble over to the right hand after two explosive steps. As the ball bounced off the ground to his right hand, he immediately dribbled between his legs, back to the left hand, followed by a crossover behind his back to the right hand. Once that three-dribble combination was done, Marcus was able to explode to his right side, like he was going for a layup.

Marcus practiced that move at least 50 times before he stopped for a drink of water.

After a three-minute break, he worked on the same drill, only this time starting on his right side. Instead of exploding to the imaginary basket with his right hand, the finish of the drill now had him accelerating with his left hand.

Marcus figured if he did something like this every morning, before he went to the school to play, he would get better every game. That afternoon would be his test.

Marcus had been at his ball-handling drills for more than two hours when his mom called him inside for lunch.

Really, it was just a peanut butter and jelly sandwich with a glass of milk, but it filled any empty spot in his stomach. It also gave him a chance to check in with his mom about Kristin.

"Mom, how's Kristin doin' today? Is she feelin' ok? Does she need me to do anything to help?"

"Everything is okay for now, Marcus," his mom replied.

"I'm taking her with me to the doctor's office. She needs a check-up to see if the baby's healthy, and if Kristin is getting the right vitamins, she and the baby will need. While we're gone, you should be able to go to the school and play some more."

"Sweet!!" he responded.

"I've been working on my ball handling. Today, I'm hoping I get to see whether my handle is better than it was yesterday."

His mom wasn't sure what a "handle" was, but she could see the excitement in Marcus' face, and in his voice.

"Your grandma shared with me a little about what happened yesterday. She said you met an older boy who talked with you about racial issues?"

"Yeah. His name is DeShaun and he shared some stuff I'd never thought about. He talked about things he has to be careful about because he's Black."

"It really made me stop and think about how I never have had to worry about those things--probably because I'm White. I don't know for sure if that's true, but it made sense to me after I thought about it for a while."

"Mom, do you think that's true, that Blacks have to think about how they live their lives in a different way than we do?"

"Sounds like a pretty important question, doesn't it?" Marcus's mom wasn't sure on where to go with her response, so she shared a personal example.

"Marcus, when I was about 15, I went on a date with an African-American guy. I'm not sure how we got together, except that we were in a couple classes together at school, and he was a really nice guy."

She continued. "This was a long time ago, and we lived in a town where people probably weren't used to the idea of interracial couples. I remember going out to eat with him once, to a burger place. And I remember pretty clearly the looks we got from other people in the restaurant. They weren't friendly looks, that much I know."

"The people working at the restaurant served us, but after they took our order, they would turn and whisper to someone else. This actually happened more than once while we were there."

"I didn't realize what was going on until a few days later when one of my friends came up to me at school and asked if it was true, that I went out to eat with a Black guy. She then told me a lot of people were talking about it, and they weren't saying nice things."

"If those looks led him to think about the world differently than I did, because he wasn't White, then I guess the answer to your question is yes. Blacks probably do see things differently than we do. And it probably is because there are a lot of people in our world who aren't comfortable with them. And what a shame that that's true."

"Marcus," his mom was focusing intently on him now.

"I want you to remember that underneath the different colored skin, or the different textures of hair we have, our insides look and work just the same. Our hearts, our lungs, our muscles, our blood types, are no different than anyone else's, whatever color they might be."

"The kindness we feel for others, the dreams we have for our children, the hunger to accomplish something important, those are the same for everybody, no matter what color their skin is. Those are dreams or qualities that all of us share with each other. We struggle to remember these truths, but recognizing them should be enough for us to see everyone as equals. It's when we start listening to people who don't see it this way that we have problems."

"And Marcus," she was strongly emphasizing her points now, "there are a lot of people who don't see everyone as equals. I don't know if this is the root of all problems between races or not, but I do know that attitude makes a lot of people see those who are different as less important or less able than they are."

"Thanks Mom," Marcus shared.

"The Black guy I talked with yesterday, DeShaun, asked me to tell every White person I could how smart, how respectful, and how kind the Black players I met are. He said he hopes if I do that, maybe more Whites will start to see Blacks differently."

"DeShaun gave you excellent advice son. Play a part in making the world a better place." His mom's faith in him made Marcus smile.

Yeah, he'd play ball today. But just as important, he'd be a support for anyone who needed it.

Chapter 24

Where is Your Voice?

After lunch, Marcus was ready to head to the playground. The time spent talking with his mom had filled him with hope. He hoped his sister and Aaron would find answers for all of the questions they had about having a baby. He hoped his mom would find help for the million different details she had to manage every day. And he hoped he'd have another great day of basketball at the middle school.

Just as with the last few days, he brought his ball with him, and he dribbled the three blocks to the school.

By this time, Marcus's comfort with the ball in his hands had become a lot like how he used to feel on his dirt-bike. He got to the point where he was confident enough to try most things on that bike--jumps, hill climbs, flat tracks, and dribbling along the sidewalk filled him with the same belief in himself.

As he reached the school and headed around toward the back, it felt a little quieter, somehow, than when he was there the last time. It wasn't that it felt strange, just different from what he noticed.

He didn't hear any kids' loud voices while they were playing soccer or baseball in the fields. He didn't even hear balls bouncing on the courts.

Coming around the back corner to the basketball courts, Marcus was caught off-guard. The only sounds he heard were angry voices.

Everyone else, the kids who'd been playing soccer and baseball earlier in the week, even the players he'd met and played basketball with, were standing, staring silently at two guys involved in some kind of conflict.

Marcus's attention focused on four players he'd never seen before. One of them, roughly 6' tall, with short, blonde hair, was standing face-to-face with Derrik, who was maybe an inch shorter.

Derrik and the taller player's faces were intense and while Marcus was still close to 30 feet away, he could see both of them were shaking, just a little, as they yelled at one another.

"We are not leaving," Derrik stated, emphatically.

"Oh, you'll leave alright, or we'll help you leave," the taller blonde guy responded.

"I don't think you understand," Derrik continued, with even more intensity.

"We were here first, and if you think you're gonna come here and intimidate any of us into backin' off and givin' you the court, you ain't thinkin' too clearly."

Derrik had been kind and patient, and quick to joke with Marcus the last few days, but now, in the face of potential conflict, he spoke with anger in his voice.

Marcus had been standing there for close to a minute when his attention finally shifted to the others.

He had already noticed the new players on the right, each of them White, and close to the same height as the player squaring off with Derrik.

On the left were the players he'd met and connected with so well the last few days. Kenny, AJ, Miles, and Valerie stood a few feet behind Derrik, each with a mixture of confusion, irritation, and frustration on their faces.

Miles, the tallest of them, was slowly shaking his head from side to side, as though he'd seen this conflict somewhere before. He was squeezing his lips together a little and looking from Derrik to the blonde player.

Valerie was the first to notice Marcus and stepped over to where he stood.

"Marcus, these four guys just showed up a couple minutes ago and started tellin' us we had to leave the court. Somethin' about them having the right to play here more than we do."

"You guys know who they are?" Marcus asked.

He didn't recognize any of them but then he'd only played here four or five times, and all within the last week.

"I don't think Derrik, Kenny, or AJ knows them, but Miles said something when they showed up. He said, 'Oh great, not this.' I didn't get a chance to ask him anything, but it sure seems like he wasn't surprised when these other guys started gettin' pushy."

"What's gonna happen?" Marcus was a little confused.

He'd seen his older brother go face-to-face with other kids, but that was different. Jason was a hothead who wouldn't back down from anyone. Even at that, Marcus had never seen his brother get into an actual fight where punches were thrown, or somebody kicked at someone else.

What he was watching now felt a little different. He realized he didn't know Derrik well enough to say how this was gonna end up.

"Would Derrik get physical with the other guy, or would he figure a peaceful way out of it?"

The whole situation was making Marcus nervous.

He could feel the tension, but when the tall blond player said, "You Black guys think you're all that. You think you're better than we are and you can do whatever you want, wherever you go," Marcus could see it intensifying. Now racial differences were in the middle of it.

Instantly, Kenny responded. "Man, why you gotta make this about race? We're here playin', tryin' to have a good time, just like anyone else, and you have to start talkin' Blacks and Whites, like we're some kinda enemy. Dang man, we're no different than you are. We just wanna play ball, just like you do."

One of the other players, a dark-haired, physical looking guy, responded with, "You guys aren't like us at all. You guys think because you're Black, you're totally better athletes. You think you own the courts wherever you go. We've dealt with that attitude too many times and that's gonna change right now."

Valerie was still standing next to Marcus, but she quickly took the big sister role.

"Marcus, you and I need to stay right here. I don't know what's gonna happen, but I don't want you or me bein' in the middle of it. You understand me?"

"I hear you Valerie, but isn't there something we can do?"

Marcus instinctively wanted to help. He didn't like the idea of doing nothing, especially with DeShaun's words from yesterday fresh in his mind. How could he help these White guys understand who the other players are, and how much they respect all people?

Miles spoke up, speaking directly to the blonde player who was face-to-face with Derrik.

"Man, I thought we figured all of this out last summer. Remember, we had the same kind of conversation, and you guys were cool with the idea of us bein' here during the day, and you guys bein' here after that. Didn't we talk about this already Zach?"

It was the first time any of the players Marcus knew addressed one of the White players by name.

"So Miles does know these guys," Marcus thought to himself. "Wonder if that'll make any difference."

"Yeah, we talked about that last summer Miles," Zach responded.

"But that was last summer. Now is now, and we're tired of havin' to work our schedule around yours, you understand?"

"Okay," Miles started. "So, how do you wanna work this out? You want us to just walk away, and let you do whatever you want? You want us to back off while you come in, actin' like you own this place and we're the uninvited guests?" It was as much a challenge as an effort to problem solve.

"Listen," Zach countered, "I'm guessin' our families have been in this neighborhood a lot longer than yours. The way I see it, this is more our park than yours. You know if this gets ugly, it's not gonna go well for you guys. We're used to things gettin' physical, you understand?" Those words were clearly meant to intimidate. And while it wasn't a direct threat, it was getting close.

"Oh no," Marcus thought. "This isn't lookin' good. The White players are clenching their fists and lookin' like they're ready to fight. I can't let this happen."

The next 15 seconds were a blur for Marcus. He remembered seeing Zach drop his basketball and shove Derrik in the chest with both hands. He remembered seeing Miles and Kenny jump forward, grabbing a hold on Derrik and yelling at the White players to stop, who responded with angry, ugly words of their own.

After that, Marcus remembers jumping into the middle of the conflict, yelling for everyone to stop.

"Wait!! Will you guys stop?"

Marcus was looking back and forth from the White players to the friends he'd made that week.

"Can't you guys see what this is doing to all of us? It makes us say and do things that don't really show who we are."

"Look," he was now talking to the White kids. "I don't know you guys but this week, I've played ball with these guys a few times and they've been so good to me. Here I am, a 12-year-old White kid from a broken home, pretty messed up about where I fit, and all these guys have done is make me feel better about myself, and not just on the court. They've been nicer to me than anybody I've ever met."

Marcus continued. "Yesterday, an older guy named DeShaun said some things, first to all of us, and then just to me on my way home, that made me start thinkin' about how Whites and Blacks interact with each other. His words made me wonder what we can do to make reality look a lot better than the ugliness we see on TV."

Zach cut in. "We know who DeShaun is and if anybody's makin' an issue out of race differences, he's it. He's the one makin' problems for others, not us."

Marcus was quick to respond. "I thought the same thing when I saw DeShaun for the first time yesterday. He was askin' Kenny, Miles and Derrik why they would waste their time with a White kid like me. He said somethin' about Whites not liking the idea of Black kids hanging with me. It made me really uncomfortable. It made all of us uncomfortable."

Marcus was now including the players he had come to know.

"Derrik actually went over to DeShaun and told him to stop makin' race an issue. Derrik stood up for me, okay?"

"But when DeShaun and his friends caught me later in the afternoon, on the sidewalk, as I was walkin' home, he talked about what happens to him pretty much every day, which is way different for me as a White kid."

"He was talkin' about how a lot of people make all kinds of assumptions about him. They think he might steal things if he's in a store, especially if he keeps his hands in his pockets. They walk to the other side of the street when they see him comin' their way. It must make them too uncomfortable. Does that ever happen to you? Do you hear people locking their doors when they see you walking down the street? How do you think that must make Black guys feel? I know none of that has ever happened to me but if it did, it would probably make me angry. I definitely wouldn't feel good about myself."

"DeShaun also asked me to do something for him. He asked me to tell every White person I talked to how smart, caring and hard-working these guys are."

Marcus was motioning toward his friends, whose faces showed deep appreciation for what this 12-year-old was willing to say.

"That's why I'm here right now, totally scared but right in the middle of this. I have to say something to you guys."

"We get stuck looking at our differences. We see dark skin, or lighter skin, we see differences in our families, or the jobs our parents have. We see the different music we listen to or how we talk differently. But if we would just stop lookin' at those outside things, we could see we're a lot more alike than different."

"I mean, think about what's going on right here. You guys love to play basketball. So do my friends. You guys are confident. So are my friends. And there's so much more we have in common with each other."

"These players, Miles, Kenny, Derrick, AJ, Valerie, each one of them is respectful, kind, and really hard working, probably just like you guys are." Marcus was talking directly to Zach now.

"Each one of these guys took me, a really messed-up White kid, and made me feel like I wasn't alone. That's maybe the most important thing anyone has done for me in as long as I can remember."

Zach was quick to respond.

"OK. You been hangin' out with these guys this week. That's great. And they've made you feel like you really mattered. Again, that's great. But that has nothin' to do with what we're dealin' with right now. We're talkin' about who has the right to be here, right now, playin' ball. That's all that matters."

He looked at Derrik, Miles, and the others, and then continued. "You see, I'm not interested in how they changed your life. I'm interested in playin' ball."

Marcus couldn't let it end at that. "Maybe it's because my family's dealin' with so many ugly things right now. Maybe it's because I wasn't sure where I was supposed to fit in. Whatever it was, these guys," Marcus looked at his new friends again, "have meant more to me than anyone I've ever connected with."

"Look," Zach continued. "I get it that you've had this great connection with these guys. And that's all good. But that doesn't matter to us right now. We came here to play ball and we're not interested in some feel-good story about how these guys changed your life. We're interested in ballin' and these guys are in the way. So that means you need to get outta the way."

Marcus was feeling a little desperate as he continued.

"But why does it have to get ugly? Why do we have to start talkin' about race? Can't we just see each other as people who want the same thing?"

Zach's intensity was rising. "Look, if we leave here now, we'll come back, and we won't be interested in talkin'."

He was looking at everyone now. "You better figure out what you're gonna do."

Chapter 25

Problem Solvers

It would be nice to say everyone cooled down, played ball, and got along. But that's not realistic when there's racial tension, and it's not the way it is in our world today. People get angry at each other because of racial differences--and so many other things--and they have a hard time gettin' past the division.

But wherever there is a problem, there's the potential for a solution. In the middle of the conflict, there was an answer, and his name was AJ.

"Hey, you guys," AJ spoke for the first time.

The White players were starting to walk away but turned around as AJ called to them.

"You may not have been thinkin' about this, but you guys want to play 4 on 4, your 4 against us right here?"

AJ continued, this time talking to Valerie and Marcus.

"V, Marcus, do you guys mind sittin' out for a game? I'd love for all of us here to play ball, but we have too many for fours."

Valerie spoke up. "We can sit AJ. Maybe we'll get in the next game."

"Cool. Thanks V. Thanks Marcus."

AJ turned back to the others and kept talking.

"Kenny, D, Miles, you guys up for some fours?"

Zach was quick to respond. "We'll play you guys. Winner keeps the court, everybody else gets out of the way."

AJ's response wasn't what he expected.

"You know, we can do that, where the loser leaves. But how 'bout we just play ball because it's what we love to do. You guys came to play. We came to play. Maybe we end up goin' two or three games to 11; maybe we end up mixin' up the teams a little after the first game. Whaddya say?"

Derrik responded to AJ's invitation. "Yeah, let's play ball."

Miles and Kenny were nodding their heads in agreement.

"Alright, we'll play." This time it was Zach and his friends who were nodding their heads.

Zach and AJ shot for outs. On the third shot, Zach hit a beautiful jumper from behind the arc, while AJ's shot bounced off the back of the rim. Marcus's friends would have to start on defense.

The game was going to be intense, what with the tension from just a few minutes ago. But within a few seconds, it changed--for the better.

Kenny was guarding a tall, slender, left-handed kid with a tough fade away jumper from the baseline.

After hitting the first shot over Kenny's outstretched hand, Kenny responded with "Sweet Shot Man!"

That compliment broke the ice. Immediately AJ and Miles followed with positive comments.

Miles said to the White kid, "Dang, tough shot you just made man."

AJ added to it with a smile and a little teasing. "Kenny, you better be careful or this guy's gonna work you."

It was exactly the shift the tension needed. Marcus's friends had shown, to him and to the White kids, that there was room for everyone to compete with and against each other without tension or ugly language.

Instead, they'd shown the other kids what it means to build bridges between people who are different than we are. They'd shown that uplifting words can change everything.

AJ especially had shown the kind of awareness that would make his parents proud, revealing a willingness to work with others instead of against them, even if they came from different homes or neighborhoods, or even races.

Marcus stood on the side of the court, watching the players competing. He loved to play and wanted to be out there, but he also knew his friends were doing something more important.

They had helped and taught him so much during the last few days. Now, their lessons were much more important than just about basketball.

What Marcus saw happen during that short time period was way beyond a game. He saw 14-year-olds dealing positively with damaging racial tensions. And he saw competitive teenagers, from different racial backgrounds, showing a willingness and ability to solve problems where everyone wins.

Chapter 26

Choosing Good

The rest of the game, and the two more that followed, between four White kids and four non-White kids, could have been a model for how different races should interact with each other--at least in a competitive situation.

The games were definitely intense. Players were going at each other hard.

They understood something more important than winning a pick-up game was at stake.

They realized that pride, racial awareness, a willingness to work with those who are different, were being tested as they set screens, drove hard to the basket, elevated for jumpers, and as they bodied up their opponent on defense.

There was some smack bein' thrown around, for sure, but there was even more encouraging going on.

As he had to begin with, AJ led through his example. After every strong play the White kids made, AJ seemed to understand the importance of words like, "Sweet Shot," or "Dang, that was a strong finish."

Marcus saw the changes in the other players' faces. He even saw Zach offering encouraging words--with Derrik--after Derrik went aggressively to the rim for a finish and a foul.

These games weren't official, and they weren't going to determine some U15 tournament championship. What they would do, instead, is positively impact eight young men's world views. In that respect, these three pickup games were some of the more important moments of the summer for every one of these players.

Marcus stood to the side, with Valerie and the other kids, maybe 20, who would have been playing soccer or baseball, if not for the earlier conflict. Now, all they wanted to do was stick around to see how this matchup would turn out. They were surprised too when what they saw was intense competition, without an ugly remark about race, or attitude, or some parent's property tax level.

Marcus stuck around for all three of the games. At the end of the third, Kenny and Derrik asked Valerie and Marcus if they'd take their places and play with AJ and Miles.

"We would love to," Valerie offered.

As the players took a quick break between games, one of the White players approached Marcus.

"How old are you again?" the player asked.

"I'm 12. I'm starting 7th grade in the fall," Marcus responded.

"I'm Jay," the other player shared.

"I just want to tell you how much I respect what you did before we started playin'. I don't know if I've ever seen someone, especially someone only 12 years old, step into the middle of a conflict like that, and say the kind of things you did. Thank you for doin' that."

Marcus was a little embarrassed, but he was also thankful.

"My mom was sayin' some of the same things just this morning. She really got me to thinking about our differences, and how they're only on the outside. I didn't know I'd have a chance to share the ideas so soon. I'm glad I did."

Jay continued. "Ya know, this coulda gotten ugly in a hurry. That's not what my parents raised me to be a part of. I think we just got caught up in some frustration, and the first thing we start thinking about is the differences between them and us. It's the race thing--again."

"We don't have to think like that. Instead, we can think about what we have in common. We love to compete and so do they. That should be enough."

"Anyway, thanks again Marcus for being willing to step in the middle of it all. It made a huge difference."

It would be nice to say Marcus, at only 12-years-old, was able to play some serious ball with the 14 and 15-year-olds. In fact, he did compete well. But Marcus's most important accomplishment on this day wasn't about basketball skills, or how tight his "handle" was. It was about honoring his mom's words by reminding the others that we are all the same where it matters: in how valuable each of us is.

The games were done for the day and everyone was ready to head home. The White players, who were ready to cause problems an hour and a half ago, now said "Thanks," and "Good games guys." Bridges had been built. Hopefully, no one would come around and try to tear them down.

Marcus picked up his ball, the same ball that only a few days ago started this life-changing journey. It was only four or five days ago he brought that ball, the gift from his grandparents, and started shooting. And it was only four or five days ago that he met AJ and Derrik.

Heading around to the front of the school and the three blocks walk back to his grandparents' house, gave Marcus the chance to think about what had happened with him. His mind was so focused on how racial ugliness had turned to healthy competition, he didn't even think about dribbling. Instead, he walked with gratitude for the chance to be a part of it all.

"None of this woulda happened if it weren't for basketball," he told himself.

"The arguing, the chance to get in the middle of it, and the way this turned out so well, all happened because of this game I love so much."

He shook his head in wonder at how a game, people coming together to compete, working with each other to succeed, instead of against each other or as a bunch of individuals, could teach him so much about the importance of sticking together, especially in the middle of hardship.

He thought about how this game he loved was teaching him what it means to bounce back from ugliness, from challenges, from confusion, and from the fear that can make each of us focus on ourselves only, instead of others.

Chapter 27

If We Stick Together--Always

As Marcus approached his grandparents' house, he saw his mom sitting on the front porch, watching the trees blow in the breeze.

He walked up to her and said, "How are you feelin' Mom?"

"I'm ok Marcus," she shared. "I'm just watching the trees bend back and forth in the wind. They got me thinking about the last couple weeks and all that's happened for our family."

"We've had a hard time since we left your dad's house, haven't we Marcus?"

"Yeah, it's been hard," Marcus replied. "But we're makin' it. I mean, I know Jason isn't with us anymore, and only God knows what he's doing; and Kristin and Aaron are gonna have some challenges, but we're still here, and we still care about each other, don't we?"

"You're right. We still care about each other, Marcus," she responded.

"We're definitely bending, just like that tree over there. The wind comes along and just pushes it so far to one side. And then when the wind stops or slows down, the tree comes back to where it started."

"Our family has been doing a lot of bending lately Marcus. I've seen an awful lot of people bend and then bounce back."

She continued. "Those examples are encouraging, but I just hope we don't end up breaking when the challenges or pressures push on us. I hope we're able to stand up straight after the wind is gone."

"Mom, today I saw something amazing. I was at the playground down at the middle school. I walked around the back and I saw my friend Derrik and a tall White kid in each other's faces, yelling. It was all about who had the right to be on the court. Their words got pretty ugly, and pretty quickly, as they started talking about racial differences."

"I was worried there would be a fight, but my friend AJ asked if everybody wanted to play basketball instead.

That question opened the chance for the White and Black players to compete against each other, and the most amazing thing happened. They started saying good things to each other as players from both teams made good plays."

"Wow! That's wonderful Marcus," his mom offered. "What did you learn from what you saw?"

"Well Mom, I thought about what you said this morning. You talked about how we see what we have in common if we stop looking at the differences."

"I actually jumped into the middle of the argument and told everybody the same thing you said. I told everyone that if we stopped seeing different colored skin, or different ways of talking, we would find that we like a lot of the same things."

"Maybe what I said helped to calm things down a little. I hope so."

"Marcus, that sounds so important, what you did. Isn't that what you said the older kid you met yesterday asked you to do? DeShaun was the name, I think."

"It was DeShaun, Mom. I want to be the one who tells as many people as possible about the great things my friends have done to help me feel better about myself and life."

"Marcus," his mom started, "I want you always to be able to play basketball, and I want you always to be able to learn from what you see and experience. I'm so happy for you."

"But I also hope what you learn can help our family. We are still going to have some challenges as we move along. Kristin and Aaron are going to need so much help from all of us. You and Maddie will grow older and have to deal with challenges as well."

"What I really hope for all of us Marcus, is that as we go along, I hope we can stick together, like the players you've come to know stick together. I hope that as the winds push us, just like the trees, and as challenges test us, we will always be able to bounce back. If we can do this, we will have a future. No matter what we've lost, we will always be able to stick together."

Epilogue

We Have to Stick Together

With so many lessons learned from basketball, and so much confidence gained while interacting with kids from different backgrounds, Marcus was ready to face an unclear future. Only 12 years old, his experiences with basketball had already prepared him for whatever his family would face.

Basketball had definitely given Marcus the ability to bounce back from disappointment, setback, defeat, or a lack of confidence. It made it possible to try again, to find grit in the face of frustration and emptiness.

But the game had done more than that for Marcus. It had helped him to see that all of us, no matter what neighborhood we come from, no matter what color our skin is, can choose to work with or encourage each other.

In our world today, we need to see that we're all on the same team: the human team. We need to stick together, seeing ourselves as only one part of something much bigger.

It could have been anything for Marcus, really, and it can be anything for any student facing obstacles. Every one of us faces or will face challenges. It may be parents separating. It may even be something as devastating as a friend catching a deadly virus and leaving this life.

Whatever the challenges are, find something that allows you to grow, to learn lessons about the life you live, and allows you to bounce back from what tries to defeat you.

It might be Chess, or dance, or drawing, or game designing, or anything else, as long as it feeds a passion you already have for something. Allow that passion to take you past the pain and past the self-doubt, past the temptation to see others as too different to mix with, to a place where you, too, become a member of the same team.

Remember this: Every one of us is stronger when we stick together.

Michael La Sage

Divorces in the US

According to 2018 CDC data, close to 4 in every 10 US marriages are ending in divorce. The most recent Census data confirm this.

But before we start feeling like marriages are heading in a more positive direction than the estimated 50% divorce rate from 30 years ago, consider this: many couples in our world today simply choose to eliminate the idea of marriage. In many attitudes, marriage is an unnecessary complication, which includes legal details, financial commitments, and often professional compromises. So while 40% of marriages ending in divorce may sound like a move in the right direction, there's an awful lot of family separation that isn't included in that stat.

When we consider what divorce can do to children and their families, we find a startling impact. According to research published in *Psychology Bulletin* at two different times, during the last 30 years, "children with divorced parents continued to score significantly lower on measures of academic achievement, conduct, psychological adjustment, self-concept, and social relations" *Psychol Bull. 1991 Jul; 110(1):26-46.*

Economic Impact of Divorce:

The children often lose economic security

1. Custodial mothers experience the loss of 25–50 percent of their pre-divorce income.

    a. Women who divorced in the past 12 months were more likely to receive public assistance than divorced men (23% versus 15%) (U.S. Census Bureau 2011).

    b. Even five years after the divorce, mothers who remain single have only risen to 94 percent of their pre-divorce income, while continuously married couples have increased their income.

    c.   In 2000, the median income of single-mother households was 47 percent that of married-couple households (<u>American Academy of Pediatrics 2003</u>).

2.   Only 50 percent of custodial mothers have child support agreements, and 25 percent of mothers who have been granted support receive no payments.

3.   Custodial fathers also experience financial loss; although they tend to recover financially more quickly and rarely receive child support.

4.   Loss of income may lead to increased work time for parents, as well as a change in residence.

5.   Children living with single mothers are much *more likely to live in poverty* than children living with both married parents (<u>Chetty et al. 2014</u>).

    a.   In 2009, children living with a divorced parent were more likely to live in a household below the poverty level (28%) compared with other children (19%) (<u>U.S. Census Bureau 2011</u>).

6.   Unmarried women are more likely to *remain in poverty* compared with married individuals and unmarried men (<u>Edwards 2014</u>).

    a.   Approximately 32.2 percent of people in single-mother families in poverty during the first two months of 2009 continued to be in poverty for 36 months. In contrast, only 18.7 percent of people in married-couple families in poverty during this same time remained in poverty for 36 months.

7.   Children living with single parents are less likely to experience upward financial mobility.

    a.   The fraction of children living in single-parent households is the strongest negative correlate of upward income mobility according to one study (<u>Chetty et al. 2014</u>).

    b.   The percentage of married families in a community also contributes to future upward economic mobility of all children in the community (<u>Chetty et al. 2014</u>).

For more information contact:

Michael La Sage
info@advbooks.com

To purchase additional copies of these books, visit our bookstore at:
www.advbookstore.com

Advantage
BOOKS

Longwood, Florida, USA
"we bring dreams to life"™
www.advbookstore.com